Choose hope and faith
over fear and doubt.

~Julie Leslie

TRUSTING IN HIM

Stories That Inspire

2017

Copyright © 2017
Tribute Publishing, LLC
Frisco, Texas

Tribute Publishing, LLC

Trusting in Him
First Edition October 2017

All Worldwide Rights Reserved
ISBN: 978-0-9982860-9-9

All Rights Reserved. No part of this book may be reproduced, stored in a retrieval system, or transmitted, in any form, or by any means, electronic, mechanical, recorded, photocopied, or otherwise, without the prior written permission of the copyright owner, except by a reviewer who may quote brief passages in a review.

In God We Trust

Trust in the LORD with all your heart,
And lean not on your own understanding;
In all your ways acknowledge Him,
And He shall direct your paths.
Proverbs 3:5-6

Contents

Prologue xi

Chapter 1 – He Heals the Brokenhearted
Ariel Youngbird 1

Chapter 2 – Keep. Getting. Up.
Adam Metzler..17

Chapter 3 – HELLP
Leisa Crocq..41

Chapter 4 – God Working Behind the Scenes
Mathew Joseph..61

Chapter 5 – #Godhears
Julie Leslie..81

Chapter 6 – The Gift of Blessing Others
Mark Brown..113

Chapter 7 – Are You Fully Equipped?
Mike Rodriguez..131

Epilogue 137

About Mike Rodriguez 139

x

Prologue

Many times I have been humbled with the opportunity to witness God's blessing and miracles. Whether in my own life or through the life of a family member, friend or someone else. I cannot and will not profess to know how or why God does what He does, He is after all, God. However, I do know that He is present and we can experience a glimpse of His love and compassion if we only get to know Him.

I decided to publish this book because I knew there were others like me who had a story to tell about God's amazing work. Others who had witnessed first-hand his blessings. Normal people like me and like you that had a story of faith to share.

The contributing authors in this book were brave enough to share their own stories and insights. They did this with the hope that other people, like you, would find something to take away. Something that would inspire you to make the important changes in your life. To understand that what you are going through does not define you, but can certainly refine you to start trusting in Him completely. You can do it; however, you must be willing to believe, accept, take action, and start living with a deeper faith. I would like to tell you that it is going to be easy, but it is not. I would like to say that there is nothing special about the contributors to this book, but that would also not be true. Yet, it would also be false for you to believe that there is nothing special about you, too.

You were created with precision, purpose, and your own unique talents. You were also given the ability to know, act on, and use those talents to become greater and stronger in your own way. Just know, remember, and most importantly believe this, "I can do all things through Christ who strengthens me." Philippians 4:13 (*NKJV*) As I always say, "Through faith and action, ALL things are possible."

Now, let's get YOU started on Trusting in Him.

Mike Rodriguez

> "If you don't know the Lord and you aren't trusting in Him, who or what are you trusting in?"
> ~Mike Rodriguez

Chapter 1

He Heals the Brokenhearted
By Ariel Youngbird

He heals the brokenhearted and binds up their wounds.
Psalm 147:3

As I have walked with the Lord, I am continually learning through His word and through experiencing Him in the still, quiet places, that He is a healer. He not only heals our physical ailments, but also our brokenness. Throughout my life, I have experienced heartbreak in a number of ways. I have walked alongside two parents who have struggled with alcohol and substance abuse; I have known heartbreak. I did not understand as I walked through each trial that the Lord intended to use each part of my testimony to bring Him glory and I pray what follows demonstrates the grace He has shown me as I have healed and am still healing from these hurts.

This story begins with a positive pregnancy test held in the hands of a fifteen-year-old girl. What confusion must have filled her mind, as she stared at those two perpendicular lines? Whenever it was discussed in later years, my mother always assured me that I was not a mistake. She reassured me

Chapter 1 – He Heals the Brokenhearted

that from the moment she knew she was pregnant, she wanted me. When it would have been easy to terminate a pregnancy, she did not do the easy thing. She did something difficult. She thought of me. She chose life. She attests that the day I was born changed her life forever. This may not seem significant to the story of my life, but trust me, it is, because from the beginning, God knew this fifteen-year-old girl would become my mother and He had a plan established for us. The plan was not established according to our wants, but what God knew we needed. And what we need most is Him. Mother called the father to share the news when she first knew she was expecting, but circumstances kept him away for the first twelve years of my life.

Mom later met someone else and he was good to us. Mom soon again found herself staring at two perpendicular lines; this time she was pregnant with a boy. Now we were a family of four and I now had a Dad. By no means were things perfect, but I have pleasant memories growing up of playing outside all day with my cousins and Sunday lunches at my great-grandparents. We were fortunate that during these early years mom stayed at home. We were afforded much of her time and affection. She took responsibility for her home and spent much time reading and playing games with her children. I remember playing with my baby dolls thinking I wanted to be just like her. She was kind and sweet and always smiled without her teeth; growing up, I did not show my teeth when I smiled either, because that is how momma did it. As a child, I had no idea how lucky I was to have such an affectionate mother.

Chapter 1 – He Heals the Brokenhearted

Growing up, I spent a lot of time with my mother's family, especially with my Grams. She would take me to church with her. I remember once while riding the school bus a classmate asked if I was a Christian. I recall not really knowing how to respond or what that meant. Little did I know, I was conversing with the preacher's daughter. I replied, "Yes, I think, I have been to church, I think I am." The answer seemed to satisfy my playmate and then we changed the subject. I do not recollect what we discussed next, but what stuck in my mind for years to come was that question. When my grandparents moved away I quit going to church, but God used the woman who lived down the street to draw me close again. She would pick me up for vacation bible school in the summer. I do not believe it was an accident that in my grandparent's absence, this woman from down the street felt it was necessary to invite me to VBS. This was the work of God early on in my life.

During my elementary school years, things were not flawless in our home. Mom and Dad fought and argued. I only recall one instance where things got physical; it was the time that Momma threw plates at Dad. I didn't see, but heard the crashing of the plates as they fell to the ground. This created an unstable foundation for me as a child. I remember one fight ending in Mom packing my brother and I in the car and we stayed overnight with Mom's friend. Mom had come home from working second shift and when she arrived, she was surprised to find that we were not in bed and were just putting on our pajamas. I can still hear their raised voices as they discussed why we were not in bed and how irresponsible it was that we had not been put to bed earlier. I think that

Chapter 1 – He Heals the Brokenhearted

was the night we left to stay with Mom's friend overnight. The next day while we were at school, things were patched up, but every fight after that had me worried that peace would not last.

Later, our family made a huge transition when we moved to Texas. The thought behind this big move was motivated by the desire to be geographically closer to my Mom's parents. The hot summers were quite an adjustment and the lack of fall and winter that used to include snowball fights and building snow men were now somewhat disappointing. Closer proximity to my grandparents meant the grandkids went to church on Sundays and Wednesdays. During those years I heard the gospel preached many times. During my repeated year of the third grade, I even echoed a prayer after our children's minister. When this news reached my Papa's ears, the baptistery was filled. Not understanding the significance of baptism for a believer, I just did what I was told, I put on a white gown, descended the stairs to the baptistery, and plugged my nose before the pastor plunged me under the water. I came back up thinking I had done what every good girl should do and proudly proclaimed I was a Christian. But it was not a genuine conversion and my baptism was a counterfeit.

In the coming years, this became evident in how my heart had not undergone any transformation. Although I might have believed I put on a good act and maybe fooled some, even myself, that question echoed in my mind… "Are you a Christian?" I would reassure myself every now and again that I know I prayed the prayer of salvation and I had

Chapter 1 – He Heals the Brokenhearted

even been baptized. But it was evident that when trials came, I produced bad fruit.

And oh did the trials come, one after another. I had no idea of the heartache that was in store. Once again, we packed up and we moved. Midway through my fourth-grade year, we uprooted and moved to central Texas. During this time, mother became detached and I remember her isolating herself to her room. I don't recall her smiling much during that time, but what I do remember is that she drank. This was by no means abnormal, however, now she drank alone. Dad was often away at work when she drank. I recall asking one time how much she drank in a week. What she replied, I cannot recollect, but she definitely tried to make it seem less significant than how much she did drink in actuality. A few weeks later when my cousins visited on a school break, one of them discovered her drink in her pillow case. When I saw the bottle hidden away from sight, I knew instantly mom had fibbed, there was a secret, and she was hiding her drinking. By the end of the school year, it had become so severe that we went to live with Grams and Papa. Mom came with us so that she might be better supervised until an opening became available at a rehab facility. Still too young to understand the urgency and the scary nature of her state, I remained blissfully ignorant. There were many days that followed that, once my eyes were opened to how sick she was, I longed for the days when I played with delight outside, completely ignorant of the pain this world caused.

One day that summer while I played outside, Momma plunged herself beneath the waters of Papa's pond. It was not out of obedience to the Lord's command to make

Chapter 1 – He Heals the Brokenhearted

public a profession of faith, and she was not going for a casual swim. However, when she attempted to hold herself under the water she professed her hopelessness. Although I did not understand why she dove under the water until years later, I knew something was not right. I quickly ran inside to signal to my Papa something was awry. This memory still haunts me today. She was in desperate need of escaping the pain, and without alcohol, she didn't know how to cope, so this is how she thought she might be able to escape. Even today as she still struggles for her sobriety, I can see she is weary and needs hope.

When Mom left for rehab, we knew the separation would only be temporary. Occasionally on weekends my grandparents would drive us down to visit Mom, but I hated visiting her there. I hated that she was not at home with us. I did not understand, when I sat in the counselor's office, what it meant when she told me my mommy was sick. How was I supposed to understand? I remember she asked me how I felt about momma being sick. All I felt at the time was confusion, why couldn't she just stop? Except that is not how addiction works; one cannot simply quit, or at least that is not how it worked for Mom. There was struggle, temptation, falling, and attempts to do better next time. As I think back, her face looked so defeated every time she fell. Because I did not understand grace, each time she fell into temptation I lost hope and I judged her. Unlike Christ, I did not have compassion for her, all I could see was my own pain and selfishly I wanted it to end.

The ideal picture I had of my mother was torn to little bits. I struggled to see her strength as she daily struggled

Chapter 1 – He Heals the Brokenhearted

with the temptation to escape and numb herself from her pain. I often asked the question, "Why could she not quit for my brother and me? Were we not good enough?"

As my childhood days came to a close, a veil was about to be ripped from my eyes too soon, it was time to grow up, and in those days, I had to grow up fast. I would never see the world the same again. We returned to central Texas as a family of four looking for what it meant to rebuild and restore what was broken. Things were good for a time, but then I discovered strange smells in my house. I had no idea what they were and when I mentioned the strange and unfamiliar smells, I was informed by an aunt that for many years my parents had struggled with addiction to crystal meth. My world was shattered. I could not comprehend these things. My parents were good people, who loved me, but this did not seem compatible with my concept of drug users. A seed of anger was planted in my heart and the bitter result was an overgrown and untended plot of resentment.

The accumulation of indignation climaxed when she abandoned me. Before she walked out, she was tucking me into bed one night and I asked her why we were going to stay with my Aunt and Uncle for a little while. She replied with these words: "Ariel, you are naive." She was right, I did not understand. When she forsook us, I cried many tears of frustrations. I was angry, hurt, and broken. I know what it feels like to be left behind. I know what it feels like to question my own worth because someone abandoned me. Sadly, I recall a time when I thought that maybe if I lost her forever, the pain would be easier to bear. At least then the pain would end, or so I thought. Unlike when Mom left for

Chapter 1 – He Heals the Brokenhearted

rehab, we did not know if this was temporary. Those seven months seemed like an eternity. Up to this point, I attempted to shield my brother's eyes from the evil I saw, but I couldn't protect him from this.

Although Mom eventually came home, things were not easily restored. Trust had been broken, and I had no clue what it meant to forgive her for the hurt she had caused. Even in the season of abandonment, the Lord did not forsake me. He provided believers to walk alongside me through my hurts. Through His people, He provided encouragement. That summer when we returned to the North, I was not certain I would ever trust her again. My high school years proved that it was difficult for me to trust. I began my freshman year at a new school and it took time to establish new friendships. I felt so lonely. I really struggled during these years with depression. I did not know who I could trust with my family secrets, so I kept them to myself, and I stored up my feelings. I could not explain why I was sad. High school is often a very confusing time for teens, and with the added stresses of coping with abandonment, reliving the fear of one of my parents leaving, and the normal stresses of being a teenager, I had a recipe for disaster. Eventually, I had had enough and after my eighteenth birthday, I moved back to central Texas. I began my senior year and once again struggled to make friends, but I drew close to my youth minister and his wife. As I watched them gracefully and honestly face hardship, I was encouraged that maybe I could do that, too. They encouraged me to attend college and to pursue a theological education.

Chapter 1 – He Heals the Brokenhearted

College began a new period of growth in my life. Convinced I could do it all on my own, I pridefully set out to begin my academic endeavors. With little support from my family, I felt like I had something to prove. Financially I began to sink and my pride prevented me from reaching out to family for help, but in God's graciousness, He generously provided for me through a close friend and her parents. I began working to make my way through college and God continued to provide for my needs. He desired to not only provide for my physical needs, but also my spiritual needs. In my first year of college, a close friend came face-to-face with the realization that she did not have a personal relationship with Christ. This seemed like an odd occurrence at our private Baptist college. As she sat in chapel, which we were required to attend three times a week, the Lord opened her eyes to see that she had never repented of her sin. This got me thinking about my own testimony. Did I truly know the Lord? Had I fully surrendered and repented of my sin, or was I just going through the motions? This question plagued me at every alter call, until one evening as I was vacuuming at work, I was listening to a sermon on the passage of Matthew 7. In the Sermon on the Mount, Jesus is preaching to a crowd and He warns the people that all who cry, 'Lord, Lord' will not enter into the kingdom of Heaven. There will be people who come before the Lord and he rejects them. They will cry out, "Did we not prophesy and do good works in your name?" My heart was struck by this admonition. The Holy Spirit convicted me and I knew I was as guilty as the people Jesus was warning on that mountain. My answer would have been much the same as those who cry out, 'Lord, Lord.' I would have responded and said something like,

Chapter 1 – He Heals the Brokenhearted

"Have I not gone to church, gone on mission trips, have I not studied at a Bible college, and have I not been good enough?" But I knew the words He would say to me in reply: "Depart from me, for I never knew you." But that is not what I wanted to hear. At this point I wept, I turned off the vacuum cleaner, and collapsed at the bottom of the stairs as I sought the forgiveness of my Savior. I asked for the forgiveness my soul craved. I began to understand my great need. When I trusted Christ, I understood that His sacrifice on the cross was completely sufficient for me and there was nothing I could add to it or take away from what He had already done for me. The love He displayed for all mankind as He died a criminal's death on my behalf and yours, finally made sense. Thankfully, the gospel story does not end there. The good news is not that our Savior is dead, but after Christ was buried, three days later He defeated death and rose from the grave. Not only are my sins forgiven, but in Christ I am a new creation, with new life, called to live according to His purposes and to live an abundant life. And that it has been.

God took an angry, bitter, and broken girl; He took that girl to the foot of the cross, where she would be changed forever. The desire of my heart is no longer to right the wrongs that have been done to me, but to allow my story to be used for His glory. He met me in my bitter state and showed me grace. My greatest desire is to see others realize the goodness of the Lord and to hear them cry out to the Lord of salvation and know that if they confess with their mouth that Jesus is Lord and believe God raised Christ from the dead, that He will meet them and extend grace to them. Was I healed instantly, and my wounds immediately

Chapter 1 – He Heals the Brokenhearted

mended? No, but as I grow in the Lord, my eyes no longer are drawn to my own wounds, but to the ones that my Savior endured to make my salvation possible. As a believer, I have endured many trials, and the scripture indicates that we will experience hardship in this life. But God has given purpose for these trials. We endure them with patience, knowing we are conformed and molded to the image of Christ. Do my wounds still sting? Occasionally, they are still painful memories of past hurts, but I bear them knowing God has a plan to use my hurts to be a comfort to others. My story is truly not my own, but one that God knew long before I was created and He wants to use it to bring Him glory. My hope and prayer is that God might receive all the glory for this story because He is the God who has healed my broken heart and binds up my wounds.

Not all things that are broken need to be thrown out, some things can be mended. But in our society, very few people practice mending broken things. Instead, we get rid of damaged things. With the Lord, this is not so. He uses the broken things of this world to display His glory. For me, I know this to be true. Currently, I am writing in a foreign country, in a city that is strange to me. God is taking my brokenness and the story of restoration in my life to inspire hope to trust Christ. This is not because of anything I have done, but because of His goodness and steadfast love that enabled me to trust Him to use my story. So, why did I go to this foreign country of Târgu Mureș, Romania? In God's wisdom, He is using my story of abandonment to relate to the abandoned and orphaned children of Romania. Through Livada, an orphan care ministry, I have had the opportunity

Chapter 1 – He Heals the Brokenhearted

to invest my life and summer into the lives of broken people. People who are in need of the same restoration I have found in my perfect Heavenly Father. My desire to serve these children originates from the love and comfort I have received in Christ. I recollect the anger I felt when my mom left, and I remember the sting of abandonment.

As I hold these precious babies and hold the little hands of forsaken children, I ask the same question, 'How could your momma leave you?' I still don't understand entirely the reasons why my momma left me, and I may never understand why these mommas left their babies, but to an extent, I understand their anger, pain, and frustration. I understand the disappointment of when you didn't come for me when I cried for you. But why is any of that important? The pain of the heartbreak I grew to know all too well has given me a desire to comfort their hurts with the only salve I know proven to heal every time. God's word is powerful, and His words are healing to broken bones. They share a story of restoration that every person that has breath is in need of. The Lord has graciously walked with me as I am still healing from wounds and He heals each new afflicted wound. In His graciousness, He has surrounded me with likeminded believers who weep with me and double my rejoicing. He has taught me in recent years that in the midst of hardship He is unchanging. How marvelous is that! God does not change, but through trials, we are refined and molded into the image of Christ. As I face difficulties, my God makes me look more like His son, if I am willing to allow these circumstances to shape me.

Chapter 1 – He Heals the Brokenhearted

Note to Mom: It took me some time to realize you were not coming home. The radiance in your eyes vanished. You became cold and sad. I have since grieved the loss of that momma knowing she is not coming home. I have wept because drugs took you away from me far too soon. But in her place, you appeared cold, hurt, broken, and sad. I will embrace you warmly, for this is the only momma I have left, and with gratitude, I thank the Lord I did not lose you completely. Although drugs and the hardships of this life took you away from me, I will spend the rest of our days together attempting to love this person who came home. In recent months, I have learned through the encouraging words of Paul to Philemon that we are to forgive those who hurt and harm us. In the situation between Philemon and Onesimus, Onesimus is the runaway slave, but Paul is pleading for Philemon to receive Onesimus back as he would receive Paul himself. Paul offers Philemon these words of encouragement in Philemon 1:15-16, "For this perhaps is why he was parted from you for a while, that you might have him back forever, no longer as a bondservant but more than a bondservant, as a beloved brother—especially to me, but how much more to you, both in the flesh and in the Lord." I hear these words, and I consider all that we have been through and I pray that one day I may be able to say, "For this perhaps is why she was parted from me for a while, that I might have her back forever, no longer as a mother but more than a mother, as a beloved sister."

Chapter 1 – He Heals the Brokenhearted

About the Author – Ariel Youngbird

Ariel is completing a degree from the Scarborough College in Fort Worth, Texas in Biblical Studies with a concentration in Family and Consumer Sciences. She is an active member at First Baptist Church Everman where she has the opportunity to serve in the nursery and on the hospitality committee. Ariel enjoys spending time with friends and investing in her closest relationships. You can often find her with coffee mug in hand enjoying Indie Folk music or exploring the back roads of Texas. Her life goal is to better understand God's love so that she might love others well.

Contact Info: Ariel.S.Youngbird@gmail.com

Chapter 1 – He Heals the Brokenhearted

Chapter 1 – He Heals the Brokenhearted

Chapter 2

Keep. Getting. Up.
By Adam Metzler

Have you ever felt like giving up? Or giving in to your situation and circumstances as it seems it will never get better? There's nothing going your way. The world would be better off without you and after all... who would really miss you anyway? Well, if you met me today at an event or just getting coffee at the local café, you'd never imagine I'm a guy that struggles with self-worth. Yeah, it's true, and in this chapter, you'll see how your adversities can be your advantage. I've heard it said, that those who seem to always help the hurting and people in need, are the ones that seem to need it themselves. It's their way of dealing with that in their own lives. *(Food for thought: when you come across that extra "helpful" person, stop to ask them sincerely how they are doing and what can you do to help them in their life. That one's free!)*

Often in my life, I've said this phrase, "Nice guys finish last," not knowing why or really what impact it had on my life as to how things frequently worked out. For example, when I was younger, dating girls was a challenge as I would many times lose out to one of the more aggressive guys that

Chapter 2 – Keep. Getting. Up.

would come in and make faster, bolder moves as I was just warming up! Or I would let others take the last of things or forgo my spot so someone else could go and enjoy whatever event was happening. Unknowingly, I was adding to my struggle with self-worth.

In this chapter, I'm going to let you into my life, my experiences that many can relate to, and how I've been able to overcome them and **Keep. Getting. Up.** I'll be sharing some of my life strategies that I practice daily in order to keep getting up when life seems to hit hard and continue to knock you down. As I look back, I see how the adversities in my life have become my advantage in dealing with situations. Also, now that I've come to know and love God, I see how He has been working through my life all along.

My story.

One time as I was on my way home, a random lady at a gas station at two in the morning, mind you, says to me, "Excuse me, God wants me to give this to you." What could that have been you ask? It was her lifelong Bible that had personal notes in it on just about every page! I insisted that I shouldn't take it, it would get lost, and that it would be better fit for someone else, but she wouldn't take it back. What did I end up doing with it? The Bible ended up under my bed and it got lost over several moves.

For a majority of my life, I've thought of myself as an 'oops baby.' At the time it sure felt like it when I was the youngest in my family by over ten years! You seem to think that you might not have been planned and that transformed into my mind that I was a mistake, feeding the inner narrative

Chapter 2 – Keep. Getting. Up.

that kept a negative mindset throughout most of my 30+ years on this planet. Not a storybook start to life if you ask me. Growing up in Minneapolis, Minnesota, my parents did the best they could with what they knew. They didn't intentionally hurt me. They didn't realize that the alcoholism, verbal abuse, marital fighting, and family discourse would greatly affect the child in their home for years to come. Things weren't all bad, let me tell you, my loving parents provided several great lessons for life and personality traits that are part of who I am today. They taught me how to be a good sport, competitive, outgoing, loving, caring, creative, and how to have fun in life with humor and a smile! Oh and some sarcasm, which I know my wife just absolutely adores about me!

    My life transformation really started when I was going through my own divorce and trying to understand my life's purpose. We had two kids, a girl and boy that were both young. Looking back, my parents were married several times. I made a personal vow in my life that I wouldn't get divorced because I saw all the difficulty in my own blended family. Then it happened to me. It was yet another low point in my life and as I was going through it, I remember telling myself that I just wouldn't get married again and that I would go through life figuring things out on my own. My ultimate plan I came up with to handle things on my own was to go back to partying and not caring anymore. After all, if I remove caring from life, what could go wrong knowing that I would never get hurt again? It seemed like a grand old plan and I was set to make the best of it! Let the fun and carefree life begin! Right?

Chapter 2 – Keep. Getting. Up.

Well, I remember one night I was at a bar with a "friend" and things were going great. The darts were flying through the air with precision and falling where I wanted them to, so I was winning and we were having a blast. The live music was amazing and setting the scene as pretty faces were walking all around. Next thing I remember I'm outside in the parking lot, pushing this guy off me as he was pushing me. We ended up scrapping on the ground for few minutes until I finally got the upper hand and tossed him off me across the asphalt! It was my "friend" I was hanging out with. At this point, I was done. I said, "I'm outta here man!" I left him on the ground, got in my car, and swiftly drove off before the bouncers or police came. While I was driving, I kept trying to think of what in the world was going on and what had just happened. As the next day rolled around, I realized that this was going to be the future of my life...how fun. *Good grief*, I thought, another disappointing episode to chalk up to this wonderful life. At this point, my mindset couldn't be farther from any hope that my life would ever turn around. At that point, I pulled up my bootstraps, hardened my heart, and prepared for the rough road ahead of heartache and headaches. I wasn't working out at the gym, and I wasn't doing any self-improvement, I wasn't eating healthy, and wasn't about to seek God or a higher power to help me. After all, I still carried a ton of resentment from my mom being 'taken away' from me. I mean, even if there was a God, he definitely wasn't interested in helping me make my life any better, so I thought.

Well, not so fast, God obviously wasn't done with me and had a plan for me, because shortly after the divorce

Chapter 2 – Keep. Getting. Up.

and those episodes, I met this girl, Jenni, who always seemed so positive and happy with her life. I remember asking her, "How are you always so happy, this life sucks!" My language was filthy, my attitude was poor and selfish, and I didn't really care what people thought of me. I wasn't all bad, there was a funny side to me, so much that I actually made others laugh, even if it was at my own self. Anyway, this girl didn't push her life views on me. She just showed up to work every day with this glow about her that was magnetic to me. At this point, I was doing my best to see through it and wait for the day when her perfect little world would come crashing down. Well, that didn't seem to happen, even after attending a funeral, she still seemed to be content with this life as it was and I wanted to know more. As I mentioned, it was magnetic – I was drawn to this contentment, peace, and happiness of life she had that I'd never seen before.

There I was, going on about my life, dealing with things the way I knew how: partying, drinking, cussing, playing softball, working, and I added a little more of that not caring sauce to spice up life. Now that I didn't care as much, I wasn't affected by things... or so I thought. The days went on and I settled into my new single life working, hanging out with my friends more, doing what I wanted to do when I wanted to do them, and seeing my two children as often as I could. My two children were the only good thing I had going. At this point in my life, it was hard to keep getting up to face the day every day... I had lost most of my hope.

Day after day went by and I kept finding myself even more attracted to this positive outlook on life that this girl

Chapter 2 – Keep. Getting. Up.

had. Then, I started to regain some hope for myself. I remember many times working a little harder, going the extra mile to impress her. Then I began to see a change in myself as well. It felt good to handle my business and it helped to have someone to enjoy it with that seemed to like me as well. We became friends and made each other laugh a lot to the point I would go out of my way to make her laugh. One time I was looking backwards being goofy, not paying attention to what I was doing or where I was going, and I ended up running straight into a stack of printers in the middle of the floor! Those boxes fell and crashed with a loud noise, and there I was, sprawled out over them laughing all the way down! How could you not laugh at yourself in this situation? There she was, looking over at me with a big smile on her glowing face. I was starting to feel good about life again, so I wanted to know more about her and this mysterious happiness she portrayed.

One day we were laying around listening to music and song after song caught my ear. I began to really like the music she was playing and asked her, "Were these songs ever on the radio? I haven't heard them and I really enjoy what I'm hearing." She mentioned, "They are not what you listen to on the radio; however, they are really good, aren't they?!" Being someone who loves good music, I instantly replied, "Yes they are, so where do you get them then?" Of course, I should have known a smart reply was coming. "From my computer," she snarked. Come to find out, these were all Christian artists singing about Jesus, loving one another, and enjoying good living. I was simply amazed, after all of what I knew of church music, as I called it, were the hymns I used

Chapter 2 – Keep. Getting. Up.

to hear back when I was a kid in Sunday school. Boring, if you asked me. I wanted nothing of that music, until I heard this. I began to download all of her playlists. That drew me even closer to her since we had the same taste in music, even Christian music, bands like RED, Skillet, TobyMac, Andy Mineo, Lecrae, KJ52, Family Force Five (All of which and more you can hear today on your phone's apps or local radio stations. Check it out).

Then, it happened, one day she invited me to church for Easter Sunday. Oh boy, this was it, time to buck up or buck off! So, I thought about it for a little while, decided to accept and asked her when was a good time to pick her up. We ended up going to church that Sunday in 2009. After that experience and the message God had for me that day, I had so many questions we literally drove around for the sunny afternoon talking. She couldn't give me the answers I wanted so desperately answered. After many years now I see why, because God has to be experienced, not explained. He is so divine and beyond words because He wants you to seek Him, to find Him. In Jeremiah 29:11-13 it says, "For I know the plans I have for you," declares the Lord, "plans to prosper you and not to harm you, plans to give you hope and a future. Then you will call on me and come and pray to me, and I will listen to you. You will seek me and find me when you seek me with all your heart." From what I could tell, God uses people to send you a message that he loves you dearly and wants you to get to know him.

Well, days went by, I struggled with this newfound relationship with God, and this girl, and my old life. Sound familiar? Many go through this phase, as I have found out,

Chapter 2 – Keep. Getting. Up.

and I was no different. After some ups and downs, there was a point, a fork in the road, where I was heading back into the old ways of my life and about to lose the very best thing that had happened to me. I needed to make a change, a bold step of faith forward, and one night at our church service it hit me like the humidity in Houston! If you have ever been here you know exactly what I'm talking about. Bam! I was in service with Jenni and we had just broken up recently. We were at church and praying for our relationship and life going forward together or not. And can I tell you that I've never felt an atmosphere so powerful in my life! It was so overwhelming I began to weep partway through the worship and then again throughout the message. That was the night the Holy Spirit really spoke to me and I actually let Him. He was working in me to let me know I was loved and created with a purpose from the Creator of all things!! My heart was beginning to be healed right then and there that night while I was standing with my wobbly knees about to give way and rivers of joyful tears streaming down my face. I was being told that we must have an open, soft, humble heart when dealing with God because he will not force His will on anyone. And that if I could do that, He would change my life for the better... for His Glory!

From that day forward the Lord set a fire inside me that will never be quenched because He is the tree and fountain of life! I am so very thankful, grateful, and humbled that He never gave up on me as he easily could have, many times, as I swore him off or what I thought I knew of him. The world has such a twisted, incorrect view and knowledge of who God really is and I fell into that trap for many, many

Chapter 2 – Keep. Getting. Up.

years of pain. So, I write this story in the hope that someone out there reading this today sees something to relate to and knows there is hope in all situations. If you are seeking hope in your life and you want to make a change today, right now, don't wait a minute longer. In the book of Revelation 21:4 it tells us how it is going to be in Heaven: "He will wipe every tear from their eyes. There will be no more death or mourning or crying or pain, for the old order of things has passed away." The only way to Heaven is through Jesus, so if you want that for your eternity, I'd like for you to right now declare something out loud, say it loud, joyful, and confident, "There is hope for me! God provides hope for me in our Lord Jesus Christ who has died for my sins and was raised from the dead to sit at the right hand of our Father in Heaven. I declare Jesus as my Lord and Savior in this moment and forever until I see him face to face. Thank you, Lord, for saving me and giving me hope and light." If you said that in your head or out loud and meant it with your heart, CONGRATULATIONS!!! You are saved and your life will never be the same - it is not always going to be easy; however, you now have your eternity set in the book of life and while in this world you will never be alone. What an awesome day!

Since that day I have been saved, Jesus has been working in my life, and as I let him and trust him to do so, I've had a new outlook on life. I've been able to let things go, forgive, love people that hurt me, and most importantly, develop a mind like Christ. A mind and mindset that all things are working for my good and His glory. That every day, everything that happens to me, I can see in a positive

Chapter 2 – Keep. Getting. Up.

light, a light that drowns out all darkness and provides hope that through it all, people will see how I live and say to themselves, "There is something different about that guy, and I really like it, I want to know more about what he has." And that if we **Keep Getting Up**, we can never lose.

Looking at things today as I sit at my desk here in Houston, Texas, if I never would have given God the chance to change my heart, impact my life for His glory, and how I see myself, I would still be a wreck. Disclaimer: I'm still humbly working through many areas of my life I want to improve and will be until Jesus calls me home. I am one that recognizes who I am in Christ and that we're not meant to do this life in our own strength. I am realizing that I'm forgiven for all of the sins of the past, present, and future as I work to live more righteously walking away from sinful ways. I now know that I have the best safety net and lifeline to call whenever good or bad is happening in my life. I want that for you, for all, and that's why I'm grateful to be blessed to have this opportunity to share my story in the hope that it positively impacts even one person's life for them to know Jesus and **Keep Getting Up**. It feels amazingly good knowing that I'm not alone in this big, fast, crazy, selfish, and broken world. It feels so good knowing that I was created uniquely, designed by the creator of this impeccable universe! It feels good knowing that we all have a purpose and are absolutely loved no matter what, unconditionally, by our Father in Heaven! Just writing this alone is giving me energy! This is especially reassuring when humans that are so close to us end up hurting us, leaving feelings of

Chapter 2 – Keep. Getting. Up.

worthlessness and inequity, when it couldn't be further from the truth.

You may be asking yourself how did this guy end up in this book and how has he been able to overcome the things in life that he has been through? It is constantly working on one main thing, mindset. It's a daily effort to improve my mindset in order to stay positive and full of energy. Life, if you let it, will zap you completely of positive thoughts and positive energy. Negativity comes from a variety of things like jealousy, envy, lack, unbelief, or your environment – those five people you spend the most time with in life. It all comes back to our mindset and how we choose to react to life, who we choose to be around, how we carry ourselves, and what we say about ourselves. Our mind is a muscle just as much as our biceps or legs and it needs to be worked out as well to become stronger. We must train our brain. 2 Corinthians 10:5 says, "We demolish arguments and every pretension that sets itself up against the knowledge of God, and we take captive every thought to make it obedient to Christ." A couple quick and simple statements I've been making for years are:

"Say it! Believe it!! Make it Happen!!!" and "Make it an Amazing Day!" I don't leave 'having a good day' to chance. I say it, believe it, and then MAKE it happen by choice and action. Never trust chance, odds aren't good enough to bet on. Trust God and what you can control: your mindset. God is good all the time, and all the time God is good.

It's said that 10% of life is what happens to you and 90% is how we react to it...and I 100% believe in that! But, you have to give 110% to this effort in order to make it work and become a habit in your life. The great aspect of this life

Chapter 2 – Keep. Getting. Up.

is we get to make those choices every day. We have the ability to choose and change just about anything in our lives that we want in order to have the life we desire. We choose to **Keep Getting Up** or to stay down. Don't leave that up to other people for your life, take actions today. Let me help. We have all these apps nowadays on our phones and devices that help us in the areas of which we want to focus on, right? Well, I have made my own APP acronym that helps me keep the right mindset in focus. In my experience, I consistently see these three principles have the most impact on my mindset, so I work on them on daily:

- Attitude
- Perspective
- Prayer

Our mindset controls how we see everything through our worldview. Our worldview is critical to our behavior towards others, our work, purpose, and most importantly, our own self-worth. Having a healthy self-worth is something I've struggled with throughout my entire life and still do to this day during moments of doubt. For me, it's been much better, mostly in part the last few years of studying and working on self-improvement and awareness. One of the main factors in my own increase of self-worth is knowing outright who I am in Christ. Before Christ, I like to call that my 'BC days,' I could only rely on what the world told me who I am. And here's a free tip, the world doesn't care about you and what you achieve or don't achieve. Shocker, I know right? Knowing about Jesus, who He is, and

Chapter 2 – Keep. Getting. Up.

what he lived for and died for, allows me to know fully what He thinks of me, which is completely loved as I am. Jeremiah 29:11 is a scripture I often remind myself of. Go ahead, look it up right now and think about what it says. I'll wait right here for you to return. (TIP: Check out what I use: the YouVersion app. Download it and reference it daily for spiritual food to strengthen your walk.)

Now, go ahead and write what it says here:

_____

_____.

Isn't that amazing to know?!

Now practice with me out loud and *Say it! Believe it!! Make it Happen!!!* GREAT! How does that feel? Amazing, right? Living your life with purpose and meaning out loud provides energy that isn't there otherwise ← another free tip if you caught that one. When you find a scripture reference, it is always a good idea to read around it for complete context, a full and true understanding of what is being said. If you keep reading to Jeremiah 29:12-13, you will see that when you call on God, he will listen to you and you will find him when you seek him with all your heart. Sometimes you have to give time to build the habits of calling on God and waiting for His answer. Don't be discouraged if His answer takes a little time, don't just seek Him out once and quit, read it out loud for 30 days making it a habit to seek him and he will reveal

Chapter 2 – Keep. Getting. Up.

himself one way or another. He wants to know you are committed and not looking for a slot machine.

One of the reasons most humans struggle in life with their self-worth, I have come to find out, is from their parents. There is no perfect handbook on how to raise children nor is there any perfect people. We all have our issues, and in many cases with the stress of raising children, we don't always handle ourselves well. Therefore, we cast our own issues onto our children, who then grow up and do the same thing with their children and so on and so on. This changes only when we realize who created us and the unconditional love God has for us who are his children. He is the parenting example we all need to learn from. "My dear brothers and sisters, take note of this: Everyone should be quick to listen, slow to speak and slow to become angry, because human anger does not produce the righteousness that God desires." James 1:19-20. Imagine living out each and every day on that one principle alone. How much peace would you gain? I am not there yet either, but I'm working on it daily and so can you. Once I started reading Scriptures that told the truth of how God really sees me (fearfully and wonderfully made), went to a healthy church, and surrounded myself with Christians that have their personal value solely based on Jesus' love for them, that was when I started to love myself and start seeing myself as worthy. After all, the Creator of the universe made me in His image!!! Wow! We're all made in His image, now try to insult that neighbor or coworker tomorrow… not so easy knowing God has a love and purpose for their life equally as yours. Scripture says, and I'm paraphrasing, these are the two greatest commandments:

Chapter 2 – Keep. Getting. Up.

Love God and love your neighbor. (Open your Bible or Youversion app to see the complete scripture in Matthew 22:36-40) In living this out daily, you automatically will follow the rest of the commandments because whoever loves God and his neighbor would not commit murder, commit adultery, steal, covet, lie, or have any other god. This is just my experience and it may not be the same for everyone. However, I will say that more and more people I meet that have a healthy view of themselves and love others usually know God. And when you look at a majority of ultra-successful people they have a high regard for God because they know they are blessed and couldn't do any of what they achieved on their own. Through daily prayer (which is simply talking with God), I have found my attitude and perspective began to change for the better.

1 ATTITUDE

To gain a positive attitude, there are a few things that I do in my daily morning routine that anyone can do, including you! What are those activities? I'm glad you asked! How I begin and end my day is very important to how I react to the good and bad situations that come up. The good things are much easier to deal with, but I will note that it is very important to praise God for them and be thankful with a grateful heart because there are things in your life that you take for granted that people all over the world pray for daily. Then there is the inevitable challenge, whether it's in regards to work, family, friends, personal improvement or something else. Here are a few ways I work to keep a positive attitude that I'd like to share with you:

Chapter 2 – Keep. Getting. Up.

Starting in the morning:

- Affirmations
- Gratitude
- Prayer
- Exercise

Have a set of positive affirmations that you can recite out loud each and every morning. Understanding my paradigm was very important to how I was thinking and the results I've been getting in life. Being a martial artist myself, I've always loved the statement 'Be like water.' Don't take life too seriously, relax and learn to be flexible, and go with the flow. Take shape to your environment and learn to relate to others to softly overcome hardships. Here are some of the daily affirmations I say to myself that you can try:

- I am thankful that the Lord has made me unique and special.
- Nobody on earth is exactly like me.
- Jesus is bigger than any obstacle I face.
- I am born and destined to win!

Another great way I keep a positive attitude is by expressing gratefulness for the blessings in my life that I otherwise can take for granted. What could we take for granted? We take for granted things like clean water, health, shelter/place to live, transportation, utilities, clothing,

Chapter 2 – Keep. Getting. Up.

family/friends, and job/work/income. People all around the world pray for the things we take for granted. By expressing your gratitude out loud, verbally, each and every day, there is a peace and happiness that comes over your mind. In my morning routine, I pray and thank God for my health, family, friends, church, finances, home, vehicles, and work. It is good to have a healthy fear of the Lord. Scripture says He who gives can taketh away and I know I'm too blessed to want any of what I have to be taken away. Plainly stated in Job 1:21, "Naked I came from my mother's womb, and naked I will depart. The Lord gave and the Lord has taken away; may the name of the Lord be praised." Praise the Lord in all circumstances.

Lastly, in my morning routine, I do my best to do some sort of exercise, even ten minutes. Start simple and slow, do 20 jumping jacks, 20 push-ups, 20 squats, and 20 crunches. It takes no more than five minutes to complete and we all have five minutes for improving our health! Make the time to do these things every morning and I guarantee you will feel better and start your day in a positively impactful way!

2 PERSPECTIVE

Having a proper perspective is key to how you act on a daily basis to the world around you. One of the things to remember is that what goes IN comes OUT. Luke 6:45, "A good man brings good things out of the good stored up in his heart, and an evil man brings evil things out of the evil stored in his heart. For the mouth speaks what the heart if

Chapter 2 – Keep. Getting. Up.

full of." Think about where you spend the majority of your day and what you spend your time listening to. Usually, a person spends a lot of time listening to the radio in their car or music through their headphones at the gym. I have found that my attitude and my perspective changes positively from my experience listening to uplifting and positive songs, messages, or podcasts. These always provide me a stronger mind to face the day and overcome whatever happens. On the radio, I tune into positive Christian stations in Houston, TX like NGEN Radio (app also available if you're not in Houston, TX.), the Word 100.7FM, and AIR1. When we listen to distasteful songs or messages, our actions tend to reflect the same bad behaviors we hear about. When we are putting positive, uplifting and inspirational songs or messages into our minds, it comes out in our actions as well! We are what we think about. Period. Let that sink in the next time you are in a funk. When I'm feeling depressed, I listen to music that reminds me to be grateful for everything I am blessed to have in my life. When I'm feeling unorganized and frazzled, I listen to leadership podcasts with insights from professionals that have action steps to improve my mess. When I'm feeling unproductive, I listen to podcasts on how to be more productive and proactive with my time management. We have a choice in life every time we don't feel well. We can keep sinking or we can **Keep Getting Up** and choose to take actions to improve our situations.

What you listen to subconsciously affects your mindset, so if you are putting garbage into your mind with music that talks about cheating, getting drunk, lusts, selfishness, and other negative thoughts, they will impact

Chapter 2 – Keep. Getting. Up.

your mind. I've found that by me making a conscious effort to see things in a more positive light, it has completely changed my life and my energy. I'm able to 'walk in someone else's shoes,' see it their way, forgive people constantly because we don't know the fight they are in. When we have the proper, positive perspective, we also attract more good things into our lives. I believe it has a lot to do with our perspective on life.

3 PRAYER

I am saving the best for last, when in reality this is the first thing we need to be doing each and every day, prayer. Growing up, I felt like I had nowhere to run, turn to, and nobody to lean on when I couldn't deal with life. People aren't always the best to rely on when we're in need. When we need an answer to life's demands or uncertainties, and even when we want to celebrate victories, we need to bring it to God. I've come to rely on him every minute of every day and that's what he wants. He wants us to depend and lean on him. He wants us to celebrate the wins with Him that he provides for us in our lives to enjoy! Make prayer a priority, not a last resort.

As a believer, I have learned to pray daily in thanks for every breath I get, every heartbeat I have, and the loved ones around me. God doesn't have to grant you another day – it is truly a blessing to be alive and have the opportunity to positively impact this world each and every day. Be in prayer for others. Praying for others and putting their needs before mine also helped create a humble heart for me. Knowing that

Chapter 2 – Keep. Getting. Up.

there are so many others going through so much worse than me puts my mind in a grateful state of being. We are created to be in relationship and fellowship with one another, especially with God. He wants to hear from us; we are His children, and who doesn't want to hear from their kids? God is the same. Hebrews 13:8 says, "Jesus Christ is the same yesterday and today and forever."

Pray daily and often. It's simply talking to him. If you have a hard time with that, next time you are alone imagine Jesus sitting next to you in the room having a conversation. If I'm alone on that one and you call me crazy, I'm ok with that because after all, I'm here to please God, not man. Galatians 1:10 is great for this. "Am I now trying to win the approval of human beings, or of God? Or am I trying to please people? If I were still trying to please people, I would not be a servant of Christ." Prayer is the best, most connected form of wireless communication; prayer never has any dead areas where there is no reception; the connection always has a full five bars! One benefit I've been able to develop through peaceful, quiet prayer, meditation, and worship with the Holy Spirit is that He sends a peace that surpasses all understanding. Please reference Philippians 4:7 where it says, "And the peace of God, which transcends all understanding, will guard your hearts and your minds in Christ Jesus."

I've lost both of my parents as a young man. My wonderful mom passed away when I was 20 years old, I didn't know Jesus then and it was the most difficult time of my life. I went on a downward spiral for a couple of years and blamed what I 'knew' or thought of a god or creator for

Chapter 2 – Keep. Getting. Up.

taking my mother away from me. Then recently, when I was 32, I lost my dad, he passed away only four months into my marriage after several difficult years of his stubbornness while his own life was falling apart. This was also very, very difficult for me, but at the same time, I was able to deal with it with more peace because I had come to know Jesus and he was comforting me through it all. Plus, God had put that amazing woman in my life, my wife, who supported me as well.

Remember back at the beginning of this chapter when I mentioned what I said often, "Nice guys finish last," well fast forward to today and I realize that we are called to be servant leaders in our own right, loving others, and shining our light into this dark world so that they can see the way, the truth, and the life.

John 14:6 Jesus answered, "I am the way and the truth and the life. No one comes to the Father except through me."

I've had my shares of ups and downs as many of us have in this life. We all have it in us to **Keep Getting Up** each and every day, but we must persevere through the adversities because, in many situations, they will become our advantage to help others. It's been my privilege to help many family, friends, and strangers deal with life's uncertainties with trust from all that I've personally been through, that I've shared with you in this chapter. So, don't downplay how your life can impact others by loving them and sharing in their pain from something similar that you've gone through yourself. Prepare your mind as I have shared with you in order to be ready and available for the amazing life and destiny God has

Chapter 2 – Keep. Getting. Up.

set for you… it's up to YOU to make the little choices each and every day to "Say it! Believe it!! And Make it Happen!!!"

God is good all the time and all the time God is good…and at work the entire time.

Extra credit – set goals and a vision for your life. Then set your personal GPS to know where you are and how you are doing to get to where you want to go in life. You only have one life to live so write it down, on paper on purpose and watch how the world makes way for those who know where they are going!

Thank you, God bless

Chapter 2 – Keep. Getting. Up.

About the Author – Adam Metzler

Adam W. Metzler is a man with a big heart that truly, authentically and genuinely wants to make a selfless, positive impact every day. He is continuously helping others with the God-given talents he's been blessed with, to add value and make life better. One quote Adam lives by is from Zig Ziglar, "You can have everything in life you want, if you will just help enough other people get what they want." Another aspect Adam delivers on a daily basis to those he influences is ENERGY, Positive Energy, and lots of it! When you are on the phone with him or in person, when he enters a room, it is instantly elevated to another level. It starts with his contagious smile and positive words of affirmation. Adam has learned to be grateful for all of the people in his life as well as all of his experiences, good and bad. A mindset he has learned is that - if you are learning, you are never losing. That mindset doesn't come without practice. Dedication. Sacrifice. He makes a commitment daily to work on his morning routine to include time for affirmations, gratefulness, and prayer! Adam believes strongly that having the right mindset and working to improve our mindset is the #1 way to a Happy and Successful life…. How does he define success? Making progress daily to live and lead a life where you operate within your passions, being grateful, and having the proper perspective. When you break it all down, it's about taking action daily toward improving yourself and Adam's life provides a great example.

Adam W. Metzler
www.AdamWMetzler.com

Chapter 2 – Keep. Getting. Up.

Chapter 3

HELLP
By Leisa Crocq

My story is one of faith and patience; perseverance and hope; purpose and love. You don't really know how strong you are, or how strong your faith is until you have gone through a trial that truly tests it all.

June 7th, 2015, did not go according to plan. It didn't even start out on the plan, but not much about the birth of my first child went according to plan. The day I became a mom is one I will never forget, but not for the reasons you might think. Actually, it is a day I don't really remember.

I don't know about you, but I am a super planner. Thankfully my husband, Chris, is the same way. Being a super planner has its drawbacks, especially when things don't go as you think they should. It can be even more stressful when it is *life* that doesn't go as planned.

I'm not sure why I had to wait until just before my fortieth birthday to finally meet "the one." But that is how my life

Chapter 3 – HELLP

played out. We got married a year later and knew we would have to fast-track having children.

I knew it would take time to get pregnant, but I really hoped that God would grant us a quick conception. Each month that passed, felt torturous. I felt *silly* in my reactions. I knew the longer it took for us, the less likely it was to happen. I was, after all, 41 years old. But we prayed earnestly and many others prayed, too.

We were ecstatic when, seven months later, we learned we would be parents. It felt like it took forever to get pregnant, though I know so many who try for years and never get that positive test result. I felt like I was fighting against all odds. In my 20's I was diagnosed with endometriosis, which is known to cause infertility. Add our ages to that, and we already had two strikes against us. We were referred to the fertility clinic just in case. As I read the information and really weighed it out, I decided that going that route was not for me. Two weeks after making that final decision, I found out I was pregnant. Finally, I would be a mom.

I'm not sure why I had to wait so long to be a mom. I don't know if there was something I was supposed to learn or move through. I guess I will never know. I try not to dwell on it now that I am a mom. But from time to time, like when I'm too tired to play with my son, the question does come up in my heart and my mind. He has energy that I barely remember having. Am I being fair to my son? Can I give him what he deserves? I wonder if I was selfish to want a child at my age.

Chapter 3 – HELLP

My pregnancy went well. I have heard bad stories from many friends about being sick for the whole pregnancy. I definitely had the first trimester nausea, but mostly I was tired the whole time. When you are AMA, (Advanced Maternal Age or over the age of 35) most medical doctors watch you closely and tell you about all the risks: higher rates of miscarriage, higher rates for Down's syndrome, and many other problems. I passed all the tests. Everything was great.

We chose not to find out what we were having. We wanted the surprise. Part of me wanted to know so I could "plan" properly, but there was something fun in waiting.

I remember the first time I heard the baby's heartbeat. I was overwhelmed. It became real to me in that moment. I was so excited and filled with joy. I called my husband and I cried. It was a miracle. The first ultrasound was even more miraculous. Everything was great!

Fast forward to Mother's Day 2015. I was 34 weeks that day. I was so excited for my first Mother's Day. I was still a mom-to-be, but truly already a mom. I couldn't wait to go to church and be prayed for and get a rose, just like all the years before when I watched in sadness and regret at my lack of children. However, that morning started out not so good. I woke up rather early, not feeling too well, like I had indigestion. I got a Tums and some sparkling water and paced around. I felt a bit better, but never good. I went back to sleep for a bit and went to church, but I really wasn't feeling great so the day was not at all how I hoped it would be.

Chapter 3 – HELLP

I felt better the next day and never really thought anything of it. My next doctor's appointment was a couple of weeks later. My doctor was a little bit concerned about my blood pressure. She sent me for some additional bloodwork and decided to see me a bit more often. My blood pressure teetered on the line between having a blood pressure problem and just being a bit high. I continued to need additional bloodwork. The doctor was checking my platelet count. I never really understood why, she never explained anything and I never thought to ask. I guess I assumed if there was a reason to be concerned, my doctor would tell me.

You hear all the "stories" of pregnant women complaining of being hot and swollen, so I never really thought anything of it. The weather had been unseasonably warm that year and I just thought it was the heat contributing to my swollen hands and feet. Little did I know that a storm was brewing underneath it all.

My last day of work was May 29th. That week I saw my doctor. She was still concerned about my blood pressure, though the results of all the extra tests were coming out okay. Still, she set up more tests. So I did more bloodwork, had another ultrasound, and then scheduled another appointment.

At the ultrasound, we learned that the baby was breech transverse, which means that the baby was lying sideways across my tummy, and not in the preferred head down position. At this point in the pregnancy, the baby should be head down. At my OB appointment the next day, my doctor advised that it would be best for me to have a C-section. I was numb and in shock. All of her reasons were valid and I

Chapter 3 – HELLP

couldn't really disagree, but once again I felt less than. I felt like I had failed. I wanted to be able to have a natural childbirth, just like my grandmothers and mother did. I wanted to have that experience that I knew would bond me to my child in a way that only a natural birth could. A bond that would be more real, more meaningful; just more. I was even a little bit scared. I reluctantly, but willingly signed all the paperwork, got all my forms that I needed to take with me everywhere, and had the plan. I would deliver by C-section in less than one week, first thing in the morning. I had so much to do in a very short time.

The first thing I had to do was call my mom and other family and friends. I felt ashamed. Like I had to give in to a C-section and I hadn't even gotten to try yet. I truly felt unworthy in that moment. June 10th would be the day.

The next few days were filled with shopping, prepping, planning, and a last date night with my husband. We did some photos and went out to dinner, then home for a movie. The next day the plan was to do some more shopping – flowers for the flower pots and some food to get prepped for the week ahead. On Sunday, I was going to plant the flowers and we would do a final clean on the house. Monday and Tuesday would then be bloodwork and relaxing.

Sunday did not stick to the plan. I woke up around 4:30 am, having that feeling of indigestion again. This time it was worse. This time the Tums and water and pacing didn't seem to help. After about an hour, I threw up. I felt better for a little bit, but we didn't think this was normal, so my husband called the labor and delivery unit for advice. They told us to come in and we would go from there. We agreed and packed

Chapter 3 – HELLP

a bag for me just in case. I hadn't done that yet because I had planned to do it later that day, after church and planting flowers. I managed to get everything I needed and we were off.

My husband drove rather fast to the hospital, which was 20 minutes away. Things had changed, I was no longer just feeling uncomfortable, I was in pain.

I was admitted and waited for a porter to take me up to labor and delivery. While waiting for the elevator, I became nauseous and had to throw up in the garbage can. I threw up once in the elevator (I had brought the garbage can with me).

I was taken to the labor and delivery triage. We gave them my paperwork and answered some questions. It was about 6:30 am.

After this, the details start to get sketchy for me, which is hard because I have always been known for my great memory of events and people.

I know that they did bloodwork. I know they gave me morphine for my pain and I was disappointed that it would take 20 minutes to kick in. I remember being told that I was going to have a C-section now (from text messages, I know this was around 8 am). I remember being told that my platelets were very low and because of that, I could not have an epidural (I would be at a very high risk for complications. With a low platelet count your blood doesn't clot well) and I would have to go under general anesthesia. The anesthesiologist explained this to me. He wore a scrub cap with Bugs Bunny on it, so we called him Dr. Bugs Bunny. I don't remember most of the other staff that helped me that

Chapter 3 – HELLP

morning. Not even the obstetrician who did my C-section. But I do remember always feeling cared for.

I would be asleep for the birth of my baby. I would miss it all. Now I felt even more like a failure. First the C-section, next not even braving the epidural, (I'm terrified of needles) and not being awake. My husband would not be allowed in the operating room because of the additional staff needed for the surgery; he also would miss it all. I took that from him.

I remember being in the OR getting prepped and asking if my husband could come in to say goodbye. It felt weird to say it that way because it wasn't goodbye. That word made it feel like I wasn't going to make it. They said of course, and I was so happy to be able to see him. It was a short visit, but I was happy for it. He was positive and supportive and I felt encouraged. He waited just outside the door and could hear everything. So he got to hear the doctor's declaration.

It had been our plan that my husband would tell me the sex of the baby at birth to make that moment more special for us, as a family. Because of the C-section, this would be easier. But I overheard my husband and a nurse talking as I was coming out of the anesthetic. So I knew before he could officially tell me.

Our son was born at 9:16 am, Sunday, June 7th, 2015. He weighed 6lbs 7oz and 19.5 inches tall. We didn't have a boy's name picked out, so this was going to take some time and thought.

I don't remember the first time I held my son, but my husband tells me I said, "My sweet boy." I have been saying

Chapter 3 – HELLP

that ever since. There is so much joy in being a mom and so much regret in how he was born. It is hard to describe the pain in my heart of not remembering, of not really being "present" in the moment. I'm sure I was, but not being able to recall the emotions and feelings of those first moments are something I won't ever get back.

I remember my mom arriving and me telling her to come and meet her new grandson. The smile on her face is one I will never forget. It was worry, concern, joy, and relief all rolled into one. She had had a 2.5-hour drive to get to us after getting a call early on a Sunday morning telling her this was happening now. My brother, sister-in-law, and 11-month-old nephew came to visit that day too. My nephew wasn't too sure of auntie. I had oxygen on, an IV in, and still had my blue hair cap on from surgery.

There were also a lot of texts and phone calls going out and coming in. I still have the phone we used that day and have all of the texts. They are a cherished memory.

We knew I would be in the hospital for a couple of days at least, so we made a plan. My mom would go back home and then come back once I was going home so she could help us out, especially now after a C-section. Everyone left, and my husband and I settled in for a bit.

I don't remember much of the rest of the day. The next thing I remember is being moved to a different room around 7 pm; I was in the ICU now.

I was having oxygen level issues and my blood pressure was quickly going from too high to too low.

Chapter 3 – HELLP

I had HELLP Syndrome, which is a type of complication from preeclampsia (high blood pressure). HELLP stands for:

H – Hemolysis, which is the breaking down of red blood cells (I received blood transfusions)

EL – Elevated Liver enzymes (Liver function deteriorates, I was jaundiced)

LP – Low Platelet count

My husband wasn't allowed in the room until I was all settled. He took that opportunity to run home for a shower and food and to get our son settled in the NICU. He was fine, but was transferred there so he would be cared for while I got the care I needed. I didn't know that they would do that and I am so thankful that this was allowed. My husband could be with me when needed, but also with our son, and Chris didn't have to take him home without me.

The ICU doctor came in and did some assessments. I had received blood and fluids. I was on magnesium sulfate to help prevent seizures, a possible complication of my high blood pressure. I had an arterial line in my left arm, a central line in my neck, plus two other IV lines. I was hooked up to monitors and was also receiving oxygen.

The chaplain came in and asked if I would like prayer. Once my husband arrived, he prayed with us. I was most concerned for Chris and his worry. I don't remember feeling scared; I just took it all in stride. I guess I truly had God's peace that surpasses understanding. I just knew I needed to get better, and somehow never doubted I would.

Chapter 3 – HELLP

At 11 pm Sunday night, I was sent for a CT scan. They were checking my liver and also decided to check my brain for any possible bleeds. During my assessment, the doctor was concerned about my ability, or rather, inability, to touch my finger to my nose. For the scan, they used a sling to move me from my bed to the CT table. I was amazed that I didn't feel pain during the process.

CT results were clear. I went back to my room and settled for the night. My husband spent the night in the NICU with our son, still without a name.

Monday morning, I was scheduled for an angiogram to try and locate the source of some internal bleeding. The hope was that they would be able to locate and fix the bleed during the angio and prevent having to open me up.

I awoke that morning to a whole lot of activity around me. I remember the porter came in to take me to the angio and I heard the doctor say, "If we don't get her pressure up, she isn't going to need angio." I was crashing. Then I heard, "We need more blood. Get the rapid infuser. Push more fluids."

I remember thinking, "Wow, it's like being on a hospital TV show." Funny what goes through your mind in the midst of a crisis. My husband says it was the pain meds.

They must have stabilized me because the next thing I remember is being in angio. During the sling transfer from my bed to the procedure table, they hooked up the sling wrong and I had never felt pain like that. I was completely squished and it was excruciating. I screamed. I yelled. I cried.

Chapter 3 – HELLP

I recall a nurse sitting by my head, talking to me, wiping my brow and just offering comfort. It was nice not to feel alone. The pain from earlier left me more than a little scared.

The angio was effective and they located the arterial bleeds and fixed them, so another hurdle was successfully surpassed. Back in my room, I remember when my husband and mom walked in. The look on their faces caused me to say a little silent prayer. I simply said, "Jesus, you are the only one who can help. Give them your peace." I knew there was nothing I could do at that point to help them, or really to help myself. I was in God's hands.

I really had no true realization of my condition. I had received ten units of blood, plus plasma and platelets, along with 20 litres of fluid. I was so "bloated" that I was bigger now than before giving birth. I had managed to avoid stretch marks during my pregnancy, but because of the rapid influx of fluids, I now had stretch marks to keep my C-section scar company.

My ICU doctor came by and joked about having a pediatric patient in the ICU. I thought he was referring to my son, and I was confused. He explained he meant me. Normally his ICU patients are seniors, so I was a refreshing change.

My husband and the NICU nurse brought my son to visit me for some skin-to-skin time. I was happy, but I felt detached. I didn't understand why, and it makes me sad to think about it. It wasn't a rejection, but I didn't feel the bond to my child that I thought I would. I blame the drugs. The NICU nurses had taken pictures of my son for me, and they

Chapter 3 – HELLP

put them up on the wall where I could see them. I was thankful for them going the extra mile for us.

Because of my inability to focus and the limited time with my son, we still had not named him at this point. I wasn't ready to name him, possibly because of the detached feelings, but again I blame the drugs. I couldn't really focus on anything and I recalled so little those days, how could I possibly name him?

A close friend of mine, who is also a nurse, came to visit that day. She did a good job of keeping a more neutral face. I didn't feel a sense of gloom when she came in. She was bright and encouraging. She later told us that we didn't fully understand how bad my condition was. Partly I think, we just weren't that worried. We had given this to God right from the very beginning, and somehow, we knew that He would see us through.

It was my desire to breastfeed my child and the lactation consultant provided a pump for me to use throughout the day to help get that going. I was so happy the staff worked with us on that and I wasn't told no for the sake of my own healing. It was such a small thing, but big at the same time.

I had a very restless night, with strange dreams and medication-induced hallucinations. The ICU room had a sliding glass door, plus a curtain that provided privacy. The curtain didn't go all the way down to the floor, so you could see the feet of those walking by. At one point in the night, I looked out towards the hall and thought I saw dogs walking by. I couldn't understand why there were dogs in the ICU. I later discerned that it was just the feet of a few people

Chapter 3 – HELLP

walking by. And those photos of my son they put on the wall, because of the angle of them, looked like monsters to me. The next day I had my husband turn them and it was better then.

Tuesday, (June 9th) things were finally improving. Chris brought our son by for a visit and declared, "It is time to name our boy." I simply said, without even thinking about it, and not having really given it much thought the past couple of days: "His name is Noah." My husband had apparently been trying out names on him earlier, and he agreed that his name was to be Noah. I added the middle names Christopher for his dad (my husband) and Allen for my dad, who is no longer with us.

I was excited to feel well enough to at least do the official Facebook post introducing everyone to our son. The replies were amazing and encouraging. Facebook had been a source of reaching out to our friends and family for their prayers during our trial and all the posts of well wishes and encouragement still make me emotional when I read them.

I got out of bed for the first time that day. I sat in the chair and had some snuggle time with Noah. It really tired me out, but at least that was the extent of the excitement that day.

I slept so amazingly that night. It was a good, deep, restorative sleep and just what I needed to really get my healing kicked into overdrive. I woke up only once, and it was to find my incredible night nurse pumping for me so I could keep that going. I was so grateful. She was a gift from God. I couldn't have asked for a better person to care for

Chapter 3 – HELLP

me. She helped me feel at ease and cared for; I regret I never got a chance to tell her thank you.

Wednesday would bring visitors and a move. Besides Chris and my mom (who were both there every day), my brother and sister-in-law came to visit that day, too. I was up in the chair and it was good to have some visitors. I think my brother was relieved to see me doing better. He had been worried and even told me not to do that to him again.

We reached a big milestone that day. I was transferred out of ICU. A major win. A testimony to the care I received, to my resolve, and to the many prayers prayed on my behalf. I was transferred back to the labor and delivery unit, as I still needed a little more time on the magnesium sulfate because that unit would be better equipped to help.

Thursday would be the biggest day yet. First, I finally got to have a shower. Though because of my limited mobility and inability to twist and turn, my husband had the unique "pleasure" of helping me. He had to do it all: wash me and my hair, dry me off, and comb my hair. It is something that bonded us in a new way, but at the same time, I felt ashamed. I just became a mom, but I couldn't even look after myself. I "subjected" him to doing things that I'm not sure he signed up for. I guess this was his chance to live the "in sickness and in health" part of our vows. I was also ashamed because for the first time I truly realized how large I was from all the fluids, how horrible I looked, and how swollen and bloated I was. I know he didn't sign up for that.

The biggest thing to happen that day was getting off the magnesium sulfate and being transferred to the post-partum

Chapter 3 – HELLP

ward for the rest of my time in the hospital. But more importantly, Thursday would be the day that I would be reunited with my son. He would be transferred from the NICU to stay with me. I was so excited. As we rolled down the hall towards him, I could already feel the emotion building inside me.

When they placed Noah in my arms, my wide awake, fully aware arms, I felt the joy that I didn't remember feeling the day he was born. The joy was overwhelming because this moment was so much more. This was the promise of our future. This was the first day of the rest of our lives. A future filled with promise that my son would not have to grow up without me. Tears of joy rolled down my cheeks.

I remember looking at him and thinking, "Of course, you are my son." And he looked at me as if to say, "Of course, you are my mom." It is a moment I will never forget.

Most post-partum patients have a chart that is just a little folder. Mine was a four-inch binder. The nurses had a lot of reading to do to get up to speed on me.

The next few days would go by quickly, but also so slowly. I had already been in the hospital a full four days and we didn't know yet when I would get to go home. As each day passed, my "cabin fever" grew.

Fast forward, to Monday, June 15th. Finally, I was going home. We were so excited to get out of there. I needed my own bed and fresh air. In our excitement, we didn't even think to take "going home from the hospital" or "arriving home for the first time" pictures. Pictures just didn't seem so important at the time.

Chapter 3 – HELLP

We had one stop to make on our way home. Ladies from our church had prepared meals for us, to save us from the work of cooking during our first few days at home. We stopped at a friend's home that lived close to the hospital to pick up the food. She came out to give me hug. We both held tight and cried. (Almost as hard as I am crying right now writing this.) She said, "It is so good to see you" and I replied, "It is good to be seen." Just one week earlier I was hanging on by a thread and a prayer.

She also said, "God must have a really big plan for him" (meaning Noah). I agreed, but what I really thought was, "God has a really big plan for me." God brought me through an incredible medical trial. I wonder what the purpose is and I try to make sense of it all, but then I just look at my son and everything else goes away.

My health continued to improve with great speed and I healed well. The only lasting issue was the medical advice (from four of my doctors) to not have any more children. I love my son so much, and in the immediate aftermath of his birth, I was pretty settled in the decision to not have more. Steps were taken to ensure that. When Noah was about 15 months old, my body was crying out to have another baby. That was and continues to be very hard. I know the risks are too high and I'm not getting any younger. I will forever miss the child I couldn't have, but it is hard to take a risk that could leave my son growing up without his mom. So I give the cry of my heart to God, trusting He has it all in His hands.

We can look back now and recognize that what I thought was normal pregnancy stuff, was not. It was actually symptoms of HELLP. I didn't know. I didn't think to

Chapter 3 – HELLP

disclose all that I was feeling physically or ask questions that might have saved me from this trial, but I didn't know.

Writing this story was a very emotional journey for me. I was surprised by how deeply it affected me, though I think about all I went through and I know I would do it all again for my sweet boy. He is two now and full of spirit and kindness and a love of music. Just the other day we showed him his first rainbow where we believe he actually saw it. I told him, "The rainbow is a symbol of God's promise to us, just like you are a symbol of God's promise."

Being a mom is so much harder than I could have imagined, though I knew it wouldn't be easy. But, the joy is also so much more than I thought. The love I have for my son overwhelms me at times. The love of a mother for her child is fierce; I understand that now. I appreciate my mom even more, and I have a better understanding of the love our Heavenly Father has for us.

No, the birth of my first child did not go according to my plans. But God has a plan for me, for my son, and for our family, and though I don't always understand or honestly agree, I know that His plans are good, His timing is perfect, and everything works out in the end.

Chapter 3 – HELLP

(Photo taken in 2016)

Chapter 3 – HELLP

About the Author – Leisa Crocq

Leisa Crocq has worked in technical sales in the oil and gas industry in Alberta, Canada for 20 years. She is a prime example of never giving up and thinking outside the box. Leisa does not have any formal training for the senior position she now holds; she started at the bottom and worked her way up through hard work and believing she could. During her tenure, she has learned that training and development are something she is passionate about and excels in. Leisa holds a Bachelor of Christian Counselling and is a Ziglar Legacy Certified speaker and trainer. She has re-discovered a desire for helping others reach their full potential. Working towards following this passion full time, Leisa has founded her speaking and training company, Radical Potential. Leisa enjoys family time, camping, crafting, all things Christmas, snowflakes, and popcorn and has discovered a new love for writing. She can't wait to start the next project. Leisa would love to help you discover your potential, purpose, and passion.

Contact her today:

leisa@radicalpotential.com
www.facebook.com/RadicalPotential

Chapter 3 – HELLP

Chapter 4

God Works Behind the Scenes
By Mathew Joseph

When we put our faith in God and become part of God's kingdom, God works behind the scenes and goes ahead of us to prepare the way and bless us with favor with both God and man. God is faithful to do the same from one generation to another. Growing up, I was always taught, "Seek first the kingdom of God and everything shall be added unto you." (Matthew 6:33) This is what we believed in as a family and still continue to do so. My parents also taught me the bible scripture from Psalms 23, "The Lord is my Shepherd, I shall not want; He makes me lie down in green pastures." He is like a good shepherd that goes ahead of the sheep and prepares the land for them to lie down and rest. We are the sheep and God is our Good Shepherd! In other words, God takes care of the hard work and toil from our everyday lives by opening up doors that we would have never dreamed of or even planned. I want to share with you several events that took place in my life the last 43 years here in United States. I am sharing these stories to build up your faith in God and to let you know that He is faithful to do the same for you in your life. He will go before you and work

Chapter 4 – God Works Behind the Scenes

behind the scenes for your good just like He did for me. Buckle up; we are going on a faith-filled journey. My prayer is that your faith will rise up within you and you will start experiencing this faith and continue to do so in ever-increasing measure in your life!

My story will not connect without some personal history and background. Our family came to the United States in 1973 when I was nine years old. Writing this, I am now 53 years of age. My parents immigrated from India to the United States with only eight dollars. Back then, an immigrant family could only bring a total of $8.00. You may ask, why only $8.00? I could never figure this one out. This was the requirement back then and maybe it was to make sure the sponsor took full responsibility of us. Sometimes it is hard to figure out why certain laws and requirement exist. We just follow the laws to make sure we don't violate them and get into trouble with the immigration authorities. We had a family from New York City that God miraculously convinced to sponsor our entire family of five. Here's the event that led the family from New York to sponsor us to come to the United States.

My dad was a production manager of Caprihans, India PVT, LTD in Bombay, (now called Mumbai) India. He was a chemistry graduate. With his God-given talents and gifting, he ended up in management ranks. He was very successful in what he did. Along with his secular job, he was also very active in the Lord's work. My dad and mom had a heart of compassion and would go all out to help people who were emotionally hurting and physically sick. Many people would come from all over India for their healing and deliverance to our apartment. After coming home from a long work day,

Chapter 4 – God Works Behind the Scenes

people needing prayer for healing were gathered at our house. He had to shift gears very quickly and had to minister to the people. On one such occasion, a person was there for special prayer as she was getting ready to travel to the United States to be with her son and family. During the time of prayer, there was a prophecy through my dad regarding her daughter-in-law. He was foreseeing a serious and critical health condition and encouraged her not to worry, that complete healing has been promised by God. The prophecy and the results came true. When the family went through this ordeal, they did not worry and experienced the peace of God. She got delivered out of the life-threatening problem very quickly. The prophecy was very accurate and because of their personal experience, the family from New York City sponsored our family to come to the United States in 1973. The reason for their sponsorship was this: the United States could benefit from and needed people like my dad who walked in the prophetic ministry to bless others. I am pretty sure that God, through the Holy Spirit and like a Good Shepherd, went before us and moved in their hearts to sponsor our family. This was the first instance where I saw God working behind the scenes for our family and also going before us and directing our paths to favor and blessings. This is how we came to the United States of America and started our lives in New York City! Yes, this is incredible! God used someone that we hardly knew and someone not even from our family to sponsor us to come to the United States of America! My dad was just helping and praying for God's people. When you minister to God's people, God moves on your behalf!

Chapter 4 – God Works Behind the Scenes

We moved to and lived in New York City from 1973 to 1978. My father worked as a New York Life Insurance agent, which took him to many cities of the United States. During his travels, he would continue to minister to people like he did in India. As he travelled, he saw many people having their own homes. My father's dream was for us to live in our own home. As he researched about home ownership, he found out that house prices were very high in New York City, while housing was very affordable in Houston. With a lot of prayer and guidance from God, we moved to Houston. My parents enrolled me in High School for Engineering Professions, where I made really good grades and graduated 3rd (top 1%) out of around 600 students. This was really great, however, my Standardized Aptitude Test (SAT) score was not that good. I scored 990 out of 1600. I was very concerned about my future and whether I would ever end up in a very good University. God had a plan, and it was amazing to see it unfolding as the days passed. He was going ahead of us and paving the way!

This is what happened on one particular day, known as Engineering Day at our school, when I was a senior in high school. Every year the university recruiters from all over the country would come and meet with the graduating seniors at our high school. There were many prestigious universities represented at our school from all over the country. I had made up my mind and was planning to apply only to universities within the state of Texas, such as University of Houston, Rice University, and Texas A&M University. I was very close to my dad and mom and in no way was I thinking about attending a university outside of Texas. As I made my way from one college recruiter's table to another, I came

Chapter 4 – God Works Behind the Scenes

across a table representing Washington University in St. Louis, MO. The recruiter behind the table was very nice and shared all the good things about Washington University and the reasons why I should consider them. I informed him about my low SAT scores to which he responded, "Don't worry about it. It is low, but your GPA is great so go ahead and apply." I was very surprised by his answer. I can now say, it was God who convinced the recruiter to consider me. He took my name and he told me to apply. I applied to University of Houston, Rice University, Texas A&M, and also Washington University. Rice University put me on a waiting list only to find out later that I was not accepted. I was accepted to University of Houston and Texas A&M and they offered me only student loans in the form of financial aid. However, this was not the case with Washington University; they not only accepted me, but also gave me a full ride scholarship for 4 years that was later extended for another year towards my Master's Degree in Mechanical Engineering. I am still at awe that I was accepted into this prestigious university with low SAT Scores. If I recollect correctly, a high percentage of incoming freshman students scored a perfect SAT score of 1600. My SAT score was only 990. This was an answer to our prayers to God. In this case, the Lord brought the recruiters to my high school to encourage me to apply at their school.

During that time period at age 17, I got my physical exam done and the doctor detected an irregular heartbeat. Upon further evaluation, I was diagnosed with a heart condition called Mitral Valve Prolapse (MVP). We were told that MVP is a condition in which the mitral valve does not close smoothly, causing abnormal heartbeats that may eventually

Chapter 4 – God Works Behind the Scenes

become life-threatening. This was a very big concern to my parents as I was planning to attend Washington University in St. Louis. They sent me with lots of prayers and support. God sustained me throughout my stay at the university and I was able to finish my higher education within five years and graduated with a Master's Degree in Mechanical Engineering. God was so faithful in also healing me of this condition a few years later after graduation.

This is how I got my healing. One day during my personal devotion, I just put my hands on my chest and I told the Lord, I believe that you have already healed me. You are Jehovah Rapha! I receive the healing, in Jesus name! One day, as I normally was accustomed to doing, upon checking my pulse on my wrist for an irregular pulse, I noticed no irregularity! To my amazement, my pulse was normal and beating regularly. Excited, I called my wife Soffee and told her all about my healing! She was also amazed, and just to be sure, we decided to go have a complete heart checkup. Praise God, the result from the heart doctor was that I had a perfectly normal and healthy heart! I knew later from reading the Word of God that the healing was already mine and God had already worked behind the scenes over 2000 years ago through His Son Jesus Christ to get me the healing and victory! It was already a done deal; I had to just receive it by faith! Since then, I have received many healings in my own personal life.

I want to now share with you how I was able to start my home inspection and consulting business. I started my career with AT&T in Naperville, Illinois in 1986 after I married Soffee. Starting a business of my own was not even in my career plans. I tried to move up within AT&T with my

Chapter 4 – God Works Behind the Scenes

own efforts and ran into several roadblocks. I felt like I was not in the network of folks that were tagged for management and promotions. They looked at me always as a technical type and not management type. Year after year, I did my best to exceed the expectations placed on me by my management team. But God had other plans for me! After about three years, my ex-boss, who had moved to Mesquite, Texas on a company transfer, offered me a job with AT&T Power Systems, also in Mesquite, Texas. He also offered me the Tier 3 relocation package that was usually given to only high-level executives within the company. Later on, I found out that I was their second choice and the reason I got the job was that the first choice candidate's wife did not want to move to Mesquite, Texas from California. I saw this as the Lord going ahead of me and working behind the scenes to get me closer to my family and loved ones.

In 1994, there was an opportunity to obtain the P.E. license in Texas without testing. This is unheard of in the professional engineering industry! Again, I saw the Lord working behind the scenes to move an organization such as the Texas Board of Professional Engineers to waive the testing for obtaining the P.E. license. This was an incredible opportunity that opened up for me. It was as if the Lord knew what I was going through. He knew that I was not able to move up within AT&T and that he needed to intervene to show me another way to bless me. The P.E. licensing would allow me to provide consulting services in the engineering field and allow me to start up my own engineering and consulting services company.

All this happened when I was working for AT&T Power Systems in Mesquite, Texas. I was not even thinking about becoming a professional engineer, let alone starting up my own business. This, I believe was another life-changing

Chapter 4 – God Works Behind the Scenes

opportunity and path the Lord opened and offered on a plate to me. I only had to fill out an official application form and submit five professional engineer's recommendations. I had to locate five professional engineers that I had interfaced with during my work with AT&T. I was able to locate them and requested of them to fill out the confidential recommendation forms and submit to the Texas Board of Professional Engineers (TBPE). I got all of my material together and the Lord put professional and caring people in my path to help me get all of the materials turned in to the TBPE.

I did receive my P.E. license and was asking God what I should do next. One day as I was reading the P.E. Magazine in the bathroom throne, a small advertisement caught my attention. This ad said, "Have you ever thought about starting your own business?" My spirit inside leaped with joy and I knew this was from God. I talked it over with Soffee and decided to pursue this opportunity. I was given real time classroom and field training for a week by a professional engineer from Denver, Colorado. He was an unbelievable individual who I believe was sent by God to move me to the next level of my career. He offered the training to me for a very reasonable amount and certified me as a Professional Engineer Home Inspector of America, an organization that he started, to help other professional engineers all over America.

I was amazed at the timing of all the events taking place in my life. The Lord opened up the door for me to start up an Engineering Home Inspection and Consulting Services business in 1994. The company name is RSH Engineering, Inc. I was doing this on a part-time basis while I was working full time for another company. When I ended up making more money working part-time for my own company than

Chapter 4 – God Works Behind the Scenes

the full-time job, I knew it was a sign from God for me to make the next move to leave and go full time with RSH Engineering, Inc. Today, as a professional engineer, I am able to charge a much higher fee for engineering consulting services.

This was God's plan and He knew that He had to move me from Naperville, Illinois to Mesquite, Texas to become a professional engineer and start my own engineering business so I can experience financial blessings! I thank God for helping me to run and manage a successful business, RSH Engineering, Inc., to this day. I am also praying that I will be able to pass this business on to my next generation.

Now, I would like to share with you some stories regarding our family life. As I mentioned earlier, I got married in 1986 to Soffee and had 4 children. Our daughters are Rebekah, Sarah and Hannah. Ten years after Hannah was born, God blessed us with Samuel, our only boy. Every man needs a son! Samuel was an answer to our prayers. I want to now share a few more instances where God went ahead and paved the way regarding all three of my daughters' way for blessings regarding their college education, especially in the area of financial blessings. It has been said that God blesses the generations of his righteous ones that follow Him.

Rebekah, my first born, always wanted to be a doctor. She is absolutely not a quitter. She will strive to achieve her goals in life. To achieve her goals, she applied to the University of Texas at Dallas for the pre-med program in Neuroscience. She was a smart kid and achieved a very good standing in her graduating class. She got accepted to the college, however, we were not sure how we would pay for her education outside of taking student loans. She applied for what is

Chapter 4 – God Works Behind the Scenes

known as a McDermott Scholarship, a prestigious scholarship. After waiting for a while she found out that she did not get the coveted scholarship. She also found out that someone who was lower in the academic ranking from her high school ended up getting selected. She was really sad. It was during this time that I had just completed my Executive MBA program at UTD, the same school Rebekah was applying for the pre-med program. As I was praying to the Lord regarding her situation, the Lord inspired me in my inner spirit and gave me the boldness to call the UTD's financial aid office to discuss why Rebekah was not chosen and what other options she had for her financial aid. To my surprise, the lady at the financial aid office was also concerned about why Rebekah did not receive the McDermott Scholarship. She then suggested to me that she was going to submit Rebekah's name for the Terry Foundation Scholarship. She comforted me, saying that she will recommend Rebekah. A few weeks later, we found out that Rebekah was chosen for this prestigious scholarship. God was now showing Himself to be strong on our behalf by continuing to bless me as well as my next generation.

After Rebekah finished her undergraduate degree at UTD in Neuroscience, she took the Medical College Admissions Test (MCAT). This is a test that is very important to get into medical school. She did not do well on the MCAT test, so she continued to pursue her Master's degree in Heath Administration so she would not lose any time in academics. She would try again for several times to get a better MCAT score. We even enrolled her in the Princeton Review program to help her to improve her MCAT Score.

Chapter 4 – God Works Behind the Scenes

It was during this time that my company RSH Engineering, Inc., was not doing well at all. As I was praying regarding my business, the Lord led me to a Craigslist ad for an adjunct professor job opening at Mountain View Community College in Dallas. I, along with another engineer, developed two courses for two semesters that year: Introduction to Engineering and Robotics. The classes were successful and the Robotics class included lab work. One day, I got the class going on their lab work and was sitting on the couch next to a coffee table. I noticed several blue books that were the same. They stood out, so I reached for one and started reading. It was a book that highlighted all of the colleges that offered Doctor of Podiatry Programs in the United States. I noticed the requirements for admission, and to my surprise, Rebekah would have easily met the requirements for admission and was well qualified for entry into this program. I brought this book home and told Rebekah to consider the Doctor of Podiatry program offered at Temple University as she was already in love with a person from the Philadelphia, Pennsylvania area. She did not take it seriously for a long time and I would remind her that there was a reason for my company not doing well for a season. The real estate industry was not doing well. My home inspection business thus was affected since fewer people were buying homes. I believe that God takes us from one place to other for a purpose, and in this case, it was to lead me to this blue book.

She continued to take the MCAT and would apply again to medical schools without any success. I reminded Rebekah again to apply at Temple University. One day, she agreed with me, applied to, and was accepted to Temple University. Another beautiful thing happened: she was in friendship with

Chapter 4 – God Works Behind the Scenes

a pastor's kid (PK) from Philadelphia and they ended up getting married! Benjamin, my son-in-law, knew back then that one of my requirements was for him to have a Master's Degree. He strategically enrolled in Graduate School and got his Master's Degree in Computer Science to improve the chances of marrying Rebekah. How wonderful is that? God knew ahead of time that she would marry someone from Philadelphia. Rebekah ended up going to Temple University in Philadelphia for her Doctorate degree! Today, she has received her Doctor of Podiatric Medicine degree and now is doing her residency in Allentown, Pennsylvania.

Sarah, my second daughter, obtained her Bachelor of Science Degree in Political Science and Master's of Science Degree in Constitutional Law from the University of Texas at Dallas. After this, she applied to and got accepted to California Western School of Law. My wife and I knew law school would be expensive and didn't know why she wanted to go to California where everything was expensive! She started schooling there and one day she posted her information and interests, including that she was a die-hard Dallas Cowboy's fan, on an online dating site. To her surprise there was someone else, who was also a die-hard Dallas Cowboy's fan, who responded to her online posting. Their relationship progressed very quickly as they fell in love. When it came to the subject of who they should marry, I had told my girls the requirement I have for them was to marry a pastor's kid who had, at a minimum, a Master's Degree.

To my surprise, Sarah called me up one day and said, "Dad, guess what, I am in love with a guy who is a pastor's kid and who has a Master's Degree in Divinity and he was a Senior Pastor at a church in Bellflower, California!" She also went

Chapter 4 – God Works Behind the Scenes

on to say, "His name is David and he is white!" For the next two weeks I could not rest and sleep! I was shocked. Why would she not marry someone from our own race? Then I reflected back on my requirements that I placed on my girls regarding marriage. I had only two requests and it did not include a specific race for their life partner. God gave me peace about this after two weeks of unrest and Godly counsel from my family members. Anyway, Sarah's law school direction was quickly re-directed to lining up with David's dream and vision, which was to serve inner city children and families. Her law school lasted only for a semester, however, she found herself a life partner according to God's plan and purpose. God was working behind the scenes to bring Sarah and Rev. David Feiser together. They later relocated to Plano, Texas where David served as the student pastor for two years at Life Point Church. Again, the Lord, through a series of tough events and seasons, has moved them from Plano, Texas to Washington, D.C. where Sarah is serving as a Recruiter for Global Mission Support and Justice Operations for International Justice Mission (IJM). Both Sarah and David have an inner peace about this direction and season of their lives as they are totally relying on God for the next steps in their lives.

The next event I want to share with you is also amazing. It just shows that God repeats the same blessings and favor to your next generation. Earlier, I shared how I ended up going to Washington University in St. Louis and now I want to share how my daughter Hannah ended up in St. Louis, one generation later! She had thought that she would go to an in-state university. Sunnyvale High School had a college fair. She was not looking for any booths besides Texas

Chapter 4 – God Works Behind the Scenes

universities. While she was walking with her best friends, an underclassman came up to them and asked if they had some gum. My daughter, Hannah, jokingly said, "No, but you should go ask her," as she pointed to a random lady at a booth nearby. He went and asked her for gum. She opened up a brand-new gum packet, and by this time, Hannah and her friends also went to her for gum. The trade-off was that they had to listen to what she had to say about Webster University. My daughter was waiting for the gum packet, but during this time she engaged in a conversation, asking if they offered the major she was interested in. Then Hannah asked her about their study abroad programs. To Hannah's surprise, Webster University in St. Louis had everything she was looking for in those categories. Then, because she had nothing to lose, she asked for a free t-shirt. The recruiter agreed to send it. She told Hannah that she would waive any of the application fees if they applied. Hannah took her e-mail address but didn't think anything of it. She was an amazing recruiter. She sent the shirt, waived the application fee, and a week or so before the Presidential Scholar Application was due, she emailed her to apply for this prestigious scholarship. The minimum ACT score requirement was 26. Hannah only had 25 for the ACT score. She had tried three times in the past to improve it and the highest she could score on it was 25. She didn't even think to apply for this reason. The recruiter informed her to still apply, even though her score did not meet their requirement. All of her teachers and references worked diligently so she could apply. Hannah received an e-mail a month or so later saying she was a finalist and was invited for an interview at Webster for the scholarship. I went with her and supported her as she had a full day of interviews. Out of 150+ finalists,

Chapter 4 – God Works Behind the Scenes

Hannah was selected for the Presidential Scholarship, which is the highest scholarship given at Webster, a private university. God was working behind the scenes again and this time in full force and might! She accepted the scholarship, they accepted all of her dual credit courses from high school, (two years worth) and she ended up being a junior when she was a freshman. This allowed her to study abroad for a year and truly become a global citizen. It allowed her to find a way to get her Master's Degree within four years and have a scholarship pay for it. She was able to graduate with a BA in Management, an MA in Human Resources Development, and a minor in Marketing Communications as well as a Certificate of Leadership. All of her credentials got her an internship at Amazon, during her first semester of her last year in school, which led to a full-time offer. While everyone was stressing about what they would do after college, she had figured it out well before anyone else. That job took her to her dream city, Seattle. Since then, she has taken a year off to work in the mission field of Mumbai, India. She is helping the International Justice Mission (IJM) with their mission of curbing and stopping human sex trafficking completely.

In conclusion, I have now been in the United States for over 43 years. God has blessed me immensely! In my life, three generations have seen and experienced the goodness and blessings of God! My wife and I are now grandparents, so the fourth generation has entered into the scene! I am not worried or concerned about the future generations. He is faithful! I can say as the Apostle Paul did in Philippians 1:6, "Being confident of this, that He who began a good work in you will carry it on to completion until the day of Christ

Chapter 4 – God Works Behind the Scenes

Jesus." He worked and continues to work behind the scenes by going before us like a good shepherd, preparing the way and making our surroundings safe, and comforting us even when we go through problems so we can lie down and rest.

I am reminded of the "Post-Turtle" picture that I recently saw on the internet. It has a turtle on top of a fence post. The world will conclude the following three things: 1) the turtle did not get up there by itself; 2) The turtle does not belong up there; and 3) The turtle does not know what to do while he's up there. Someone had to place the turtle on top of the post. The turtle cannot, by itself, climb up to the top of the post. That's the way it has been in my life. The goodness and faithfulness of God has placed my family and me on top of many life posts! I call them God-ordained posts. When He places us there, He equips us with all the proper tools necessary to stay up there for a season of our life. He places us at the right place at the right time for the right purpose. And whenever someone asks me about a post my family and I are sitting upon, I will say, "It's all God and God placed us there on top of the post! I know God can take you and your life and position you on top of the post, just like the turtle. As God goes ahead of you, my prayer is that He will be placing you on these God-ordained posts of life so you can also say with me, "God is a good, God who is working behind the scenes for my good!"

Chapter 4 – God Works Behind the Scenes

About the Author – Mathew Joseph

Mathew Joseph is married to Sweet Soffee and has been blessed with four children that he calls: Remarkable Rebekah, Smiling Sarah, Happy Hannah, and Sharp Samuel and two Super son-in-law's, Ben and David and two grandchildren, Joseph and Luke.

Mathew Joseph received his Bachelor's and Master's degree in Mechanical Engineering from Washington University in St. Louis, Missouri, and Master's in Business Administration from University of Texas at Dallas. He is also a Licensed Professional Engineer with the State of Texas. As an entrepreneur, he and his wife founded RSH Engineering, Inc. in 1994, a successful and thriving business in Dallas, Texas. He presently serves as the CEO and Principal Consultant. His vast experience spans multiple disciplines: Product Design, Process Engineering, Product Safety, Cost Reduction, Residential Home and Commercial Real Estate Inspector and Forensic Engineering. He has worked in the Telecommunication industry.

He is a graduate of the Church of God Ministerial Internship Program and currently is an Ordained Minister with the Assemblies of God and serves as Associate Pastor at Heavenly Call Missions Church in Dallas, Texas. He is a lay

Chapter 4 – God Works Behind the Scenes

counselor certified by American Association of Christian Counselors. He is also a father, husband, mentor, servant leader, and gifted speaker. His passion is to remind and let people know about their identity in Christ and to see them live their lives to the fullest God-given potential!

Rev. Mathew Joseph
(972) 523-5746
president@rshengineering.com
http://www.rshengineering.com

Chapter 4 – God Works Behind the Scenes

Chapter 4 – God Works Behind the Scenes

Chapter 5

#Godhears
By Julie Leslie

That I even went to this doctor's appointment with my husband Gary was perhaps the first of many miracles we would experience. It was a sweltering August day and Gary had a 4:00 p.m. appointment to learn the results of additional bloodwork and scans he had done earlier in the week in response to elevated liver enzymes found during a routine physical.

The feeling that I should go to this appointment with him had nagged at me all day, but I tried to ignore it. I was scheduled to be in a meeting until 4:30 and felt obligated to attend. "We Googled this," I reasoned to myself. "All of his symptoms line up with gallstones, which isn't a big deal. It's not serious." His mom, aunt, and sister all had their gallbladders removed over the years, so this was a logical conclusion. Still, the nagging feeling persisted. I ignored it, though, and tried to focus on my colleagues and our discussion.

At 3:30 our meeting was interrupted, which was highly unusual. Due to a scheduling conflict, another group was waiting to use this large conference room, so our meeting abruptly ended. As my colleagues and I quickly gathered up

Chapter 5 – #Godhears

our laptops and papers, my mind raced. Maybe I could leave early! I could go with Gary after all! Thankfully my director, a woman I adore, was in the group waiting outside the door, so I got her blessing to leave early. I flew down three flights of stairs, tossed my bags in the backseat, and squealed out of the parking lot. The time was 3:40. I'd be late, but I could still make it.

****

We ended up waiting nearly an hour to see the doctor, first in the waiting room and then in an exam room. (We now know that he wanted Gary to be his last patient of the day.) Finally, the doctor walked in with Gary's file, and I'll never forget that conversation. A former Special Ops Medic in the US Army, this doctor bears the scars from bloodshed and battle. He got straight to the point.

"There's no good way to say this, so I'm just going to say it: you have pancreatic cancer."

"What?" Gary asked. He blinked in confusion. "What did you say?"

"You have pancreatic cancer," the doctor repeated in a softer tone. "You have a tumor on your pancreas, and so the chances are very good that you have cancer. These things are almost never benign."

I recall so vividly – even in my complete disbelief – Gary holding up the piece of paper on which he'd listed all the symptoms for gallstones and saying, "But my symptoms are on the list for gallstones…" and the doctor's response, "Yes. But those are *also* symptoms of pancreatic cancer. You didn't know to Google pancreatic cancer." Gary just stared at the doctor. And me? I couldn't quit staring at that stupid piece of paper Gary continued to hold up. I was seeing the list,

Chapter 5 – #Godhears

Gary's strong hand, and his wedding ring all at once in a beautiful, obscene image that defined this devastating moment.

Silence.

I couldn't speak.

Then Gary asked, "Now what?"

"Two things," the doctor answered. "The first is don't wait. You'll be sad and maybe even angry, but don't be in denial. Pancreatic cancer is too aggressive and deadly. Here's the number of an oncologist. Get in his office. TOMORROW. I'm sending your test results over there tonight."

"Alright," Gary responded. "What's the other thing?"

"Don't Google pancreatic cancer." The doctor looked straight at me. "I know you. The first thing you're gonna want to do is go home and research this on the internet. I strongly advise against doing that. You'll get lost in a hurry in all the technical stuff, and the numbers will paralyze you with fear. You absolutely cannot get paralyzed or be in denial. You've got to MOVE on this. Tonight, you can go out and eat a big steak, or go home and cry. Or both. Do what you've gotta do tonight, but tomorrow? *Tomorrow you MOVE.*"

I froze. Not usually at a loss for words, I couldn't speak. Neither of us had ever heard a doctor talk like this before. All we could do was shake our heads in agreement. We sat there in silence, the three of us, in that sterile room. Time seemed to stand still, yet I recall hearing the clock tick.

Chapter 5 – #Godhears

Finally, my brave husband spoke, "So, what *are* the numbers?"

More silence.

The doctor took a deep breath, "One stat is 1 in 20. 1 in 20 live five or more years after being diagnosed." His face was solemn.

Gary quickly did the math, "That's 5%."

"Yes. I've seen another statistic that's 8%. But there are many variables that we don't know yet, including if the cancer has spread and the exact location of the tumor relative to a major vein. This is why I told you not to Google this tonight. There are still too many things you don't know. You're young for a typical pancreatic cancer patient, and you're in otherwise great health. Those two things are huge. But this is why you've got to move fast."

We were totally and completely SHOCKED. Speechless. We sat in silence again. Finally, Gary and I stood together and walked hand-in-hand out of the doctor's office. Upon reaching the parking lot, we clung to each other and sobbed. We finally got in our cars and started driving home. In my rearview mirror, I could see Gary talking on the phone, so I called my sister. As soon as I heard her voice, I started sobbing again. I could barely speak. When Gary and I got home, we clung to each other again and wept some more.

When we couldn't cry anymore, we started talking. We talked into the night, and we made two very important decisions: to trust God and to fight this battle together. I promised Gary I'd be beside him every step of the way – that I'd go to every doctor's appointment with him and that I'd do whatever it took to care for him during chemo. "We'll handle this together. Whatever is coming, we'll face it together."

Chapter 5 – #Godhears

I fell asleep that night praying for strength and courage. I had never been so afraid. I was so, so afraid.

Early the next morning, my older brother David called me. It was good to hear his voice. "Julie," I heard him say, "Diane called me last night and told me the news. How are you?"

"I don't know yet." I exhaled. "I'm sittin' here having a cup of coffee just like any other morning. Except it's not any other morning. It's day one. And I have no idea what to do. This is just so out of left field." Quiet tears slid down my cheeks.

"You've got to figure it out," Dave said. "And you will." For a few moments neither of us said anything. Then, as only brothers can do, he continued with serious conviction, "Now listen to me, Julie. You're a Buckler, and Bucklers are strong. When life is hard, we pray about it and we fight. You know that. You've gotta be strong for Gary and charge ahead! Take one hurdle at a time. Get over it, around it, under it, or through it, but master that hurdle and tackle the next one. Take it one hurdle at a time. But you need to quit your crying and step up. Gary's gonna need you."

"I know, I know," I answered quietly. "I will. I can't imagine how yet, but I will."

"You *will*," Dave responded. "I love you, Jul. Now, don't forget! Charge ahead!" We hung up, and I watched a cardinal splashing in the birdbath. "You're a Buckler," Dave had said. Those words rang in my ears. That made me think of our father, John Buckler. He was a tough Marine who'd eventually succumbed to bone cancer, but his faith never faltered. All throughout my life, he had consistently modeled love for our mother and faith in God. I saw him countless times during my childhood and teen years literally praying on his knees at his bedside. He did that every night until he

Chapter 5 – #Godhears

couldn't at the end. He modeled integrity, perseverance, and backbone, yet he was tender with me at all the right times. "A Buckler," I thought.

"Charge ahead!" Dave had also said. It was sage advice, but I wondered how I would do that. This, too, reminded me of our Marine father and how he'd fought bravely in the Korean War. How he'd thrashed violently in bed from nightmares for months after returning. How he had scars he never complained about or even spoke of. What would "charging ahead" look like for him? I thought I knew. But, for me? I had no idea.

After some time, I wiped my cheeks and called the local oncology center where Gary's test results had been sent. The date was Tuesday, August 16, 2016.

****

Things happened fast after that, but we kept the news very quiet at first. Only immediate family members, a few close friends, and a small circle of my colleagues knew, and this was purposeful. We needed all of our emotional energy and time for digesting this new, complicated medical information and for creating a game plan. Had we posted this on social media and rallied prayer chains right away, many people would have called and texted. Responding would have been a distraction we couldn't afford. Gary was growing sicker by the day, and I was busy helping him, making appointments, and panicking about whether I knew all of our passwords. Gary and I decided we would get more information and only then would we notify others. While I know it seemed to some like we were being secretive, that wasn't it. Grappling with our new reality – cancer – was exhausting and hard. It required all we had. Others would have to wait.

Chapter 5 – #Godhears

After several weeks, one of Gary's sisters created a private social media group that helped me communicate with more people in less time. This was a big help.

Gary and I did see a local oncologist, but we quickly realized we wanted a second opinion for a diagnosis this life-threatening. Thankfully, a family friend knew of an outstanding surgical oncologist – referred to here as Dr. Awesome – who specializes in pancreatic and digestive cancers at a world-renowned research hospital in Dallas. If being with Gary when he was told he had pancreatic cancer was Miracle #1, that Gary got an appointment with Dr. Awesome's medical team was Miracle #2. It gave us much-needed confidence that this team approached each pancreatic cancer patient as just that – a team. Gary would see surgical and medical oncologists on the same day, and then they would join several other doctors in a joint meeting to determine the best treatment plan. We were grateful that the team could see Gary within a week's time, however, getting an appointment that soon meant Gary would have a different surgeon. While we were disappointed that Dr. Awesome wouldn't be Gary's surgeon, every surgeon on the team had an outstanding resume, so we agreed to a different surgeon. Plus, we believed that even one day could be a game-changer.

We physically drove Gary's CT scans and blood work results into Dallas to keep things moving quickly. I left Gary in the car and walked into that huge facility. I had no idea where to go, but I knew I had to find that office and put Gary's results in exactly the right hands. I believed his life depended on it. Again, I was so afraid. Doubt crept in. "What if I can't find the exact nurse I'm supposed to give these to in this huge hospital? What if she's already gone home for the day? It's almost the weekend." I've done so many things while being

Chapter 5 – #Godhears

afraid in the past year, and this was one of the first. I finally found this nurse and said a prayer as I handed her Gary's results.

By Saturday night, Gary's physical symptoms had worsened significantly. He couldn't eat, he was lethargic, and he was becoming more and more jaundiced. The whites of his eyes and his skin tone were so yellow it was downright eerie. I drove him back into Dallas to this same hospital's emergency room. If Gary needed to be hospitalized, we wanted to be at the same hospital as this specialized oncology team.

More tests revealed that Gary's tumor was blocking a duct that runs between the liver and the pancreas. His liver couldn't drain properly, and this was the cause of Gary's fatigue and other symptoms that made him go in for the routine physical three weeks earlier. The tumor had also caused Gary's blood work to come back with elevated liver enzymes, which is why the doctor ordered the CT scan that ultimately found the tumor. We would come to believe that the tumor's location – by causing warning symptoms like elevated liver enzymes – was Miracle #3. At the moment, Gary's liver was in extreme crisis. Things were going from bad to worse in a hurry.

Much to our relief, the ER doctors were able to stabilize Gary's liver so that he could wait two days for a stent to be inserted in the duct that was being blocked by the tumor and allow this duct to drain the liver properly again. The procedure to insert the stent was described as "routine," but it sure sounded complicated and rife with ways for things to go wrong. Guided by a skilled surgeon, a device that held both a camera and the stent (which looks like chain link fence, is an inch long, and as big around as a pencil) was put down Gary's throat, wound all the way through his stomach and the first part of his small intestine, and was eventually put into place thereby opening up the blocked biliary duct. The procedure was successful, and Gary's color began returning to normal almost immediately. Serious as this sounds, it's a day procedure. Gary and I were home by late afternoon, but by 10:00 p.m. he was in severe pain. The surgeon had us take some over-the-counter medicine, but it did little. By early morning we knew something was terribly wrong and headed back down to the ER. The diagnosis? Pancreatitis, which was described to us as "basically the pancreas gets really angry and begins digesting itself." Six days ago, we barely even knew we had a pancreas, and now it was driving everything.

In situations like this, doctors and nurses ask the patient to describe pain on a 1-10 scale with 10 being the absolute worst. Gary was hospitalized for six days with pancreatitis and put his pain at a 9 or 10 for some of that time. Ten pounds melted away from his muscular frame, and he spoke little. I stayed with him night and day, assisting the nurses when possible and fretting over pretty much everything. When he rested, I frantically responded to text messages and initiated a few more, asking for prayers from people I know are prayer warriors. I prayed a lot myself, too, though talking to God for any length of time made me weep. During these prayers, I felt really loved by God.

Held.

Carried.

In His powerful grip.

But, I also felt REALLY afraid. I knew intellectually that God was in control, but at the same time, I was watching my powerful man fight for his life. I recall being so grateful for every text and Facebook post telling me that people were praying for Gary and that he'd been added to their church or

Chapter 5 – #Godhears

home group's prayer list. "God hears," I told myself over and over. "God hears." Still, fear had a strangulation hold around my very neck. I could hardly breathe. My rib cage, shoulders, and neck were tense and sore because I kept holding my breath. I knew I had to get a handle on this fear, but I didn't have time to think about how to do that. Yet.

Because of this week-long hospital stay due to pancreatitis, Gary missed his appointment with the oncology team that would determine his cancer treatment plan. When this team called me with the new appointment date, I could hardly believe my ears. The delay put Gary back on Dr. Awesome's schedule! He would be Gary's surgeon after all! Unbelievably, the latest miracle had come disguised as something as scary and painful as pancreatitis. Gary was still in the hospital at this time, but we were greatly encouraged. Yes, it sure did seem like God hears.

Gary was only out of the hospital for a few days when we drove back into Dallas to meet with Dr. Awesome and various other doctors to learn more about the tumor's location, the stage of the cancer, if it had spread to other major organs, and the overall treatment plan. Even though he was still weak from his ordeal with pancreatitis, Gary had an iron grip on my hand as we walked up the long sidewalk and into that hospital building. Overall the news was mixed – some parts positive, some parts worrisome. The cancer was considered Stage 2 because it hadn't spread to the liver, lungs, stomach, or spine, so that was excellent news. However, the doctors weren't sure the tumor was operable. The tumor was dangerously close to a major vein that runs through the digestive system, and this vein can't be cut. We were told that Gary's only chance at long-term survival hinged on <u>IF</u> the tumor responded to chemotherapy and, later on, <u>IF</u> the surgeon could fully remove the tumor.

Chapter 5 – #Godhears

Gary would be on three strong chemo drugs in an effort to get that tumor to pull away from the vein enough for the surgeon to remove it. Everything hinged on the success of the chemo. And the chemo would be brutal.

The next morning found me in the same chair as before, staring at the same birdbath, perhaps even staring at the same cardinal as he happily splashed in the water. Gary was still in bed, but I had awakened early. As I sat there with my coffee, silently talking to God, I believe He sent me an image in the form of a daydream. I had been praying for strength and courage, and I believe this daydream was an answer to that prayer. In my daydream, Gary and I were walking hand-in-hand along a manicured, narrow path that was only wide enough for our passage. There was a tall hedge on both sides that reached all the way to the sky, which was blue with puffy, white clouds. The sides of this hedge were dark, but not in an evil, scary way. They were just dark, tight, and thick. Walking ahead of us was a tall man. I could only see his silhouette from the back. He was broad-shouldered, muscular, and much taller than us. The sun was bright, but this man's body shielded us from the brightness. I couldn't see what was ahead of the man, but he was wielding a huge sword and was slashing to the right and to the left to create a path for Gary and me. In my daydream, Gary and I walked steadily and at a good pace with this man going before us. I can't really describe the sense of peace that overwhelmed me in that moment. I knew the man was Jesus and that He was going before us in this battle! Suddenly, it seemed possible to triumph in this tragic situation. I felt a growing confidence that I would describe as a "peace that surpasses all understanding" given the seriousness of the situation.

The image of Jesus as our Mighty Warrior in my daydream, along with my brother's admonition to quit crying and

Chapter 5 – #Godhears

"Charge ahead!", gave me the beginning of a strategy I needed to deal with my fear and to best help my husband. We'd determined that first night to fight this thing together, but in the days after I had to remind myself many times to focus on hope. Being brave doesn't mean you're not afraid – it means you find a way to put fear in perspective and not be paralyzed by it. Together we had to fight! Gary's fight would be both physical and emotional. It would take tremendous willpower. Mine would be physical, too, in that I wouldn't get a lot of rest, but it would be mostly emotional. That morning's daydream gave me a breakthrough in my thinking – we would have to go on offense. We would need to meet this cruel disease on the battlefield. Every single day. We would need to ACT. Not just RE-act. *PRO*-act. What this would look like day to day wasn't clear yet, but I had the beginning of a strategy. This wouldn't be just about defense. We would need to go on offense, too. We would need to attack. And what came with this breakthrough? HOPE.

It's a good thing, too. We would need it.

Chemo was indeed brutal, especially the first two treatments. During the first one, I helped Gary get into bed. He was shaking, nauseated, and weak. As I gently pulled a blanket up over his shoulders and got him tucked in, he whispered, "If this is how chemo is every time, I don't know how people survive it." I was nearly undone.

During September and October's chemo treatments, Gary received three extremely strong drugs over a three-day period. The first two drugs were given at the hospital on a Wednesday and took three or four hours to infuse into his system. Then he was sent home with a pump that would inject the third drug on a slow drip over the next 46 hours. Put another way, Gary got strong chemo for three straight days. We would return to the hospital on Friday for him to

Chapter 5 – #Godhears

be disconnected from the pump. The drive home on Wednesday - and then the drive to and from Dallas on Friday - was hard. Gary was so sick. It was nerve-wracking to drive in traffic on busy highways that had parts under construction with such a fragile, precious passenger.

It would take him more than a week to recover from these chemo rounds. Just when he would start feeling better, it was time to go back again. There were times when my strong man needed a wheelchair to get from the car to the infusion room. I marveled at his will to live! He fought to keep food down and had no appetite, but he had to eat and drink. Lightheadedness and fainting due to dehydration were constant threats, so there were days when he didn't leave the bedroom without carrying a tall garbage can – either to vomit in or to catch himself. Sometimes both. During one chemo infusion, he developed tics in his eyelids. He couldn't feel these, but they were noticeable to me and unnerving to look at. Sometimes he would also get these micro-spasms in his leg muscles, and they, too, were frightening. It looked like tiny, super-fast bugs were skittering just under his skin. One night he had chest pressure and muscle spasms that caused us grave concern. I wondered if he was having a heart attack. While I followed the doctor's advice and didn't Google much related to pancreatic cancer, I sat on the edge of the bathtub that night and Googled the chemo drugs Gary was on. Much to my relief, one hit described side effects like Gary was experiencing. The article said chest pain and spasms occur in a small percentage of patients, so I decided that Gary wasn't having a heart attack and put him back to bed. I got dressed just in case I had to rush him to the ER after all and waited for dawn, watching him in the soft glow of the bathroom light.

Chapter 5 – #Godhears

On infusion days and for several days thereafter, when he was sleeping, I would steal into our bedroom every half hour and stare at his legs to see if these micro-spasms were increasing in number or duration. Sometimes I would delicately rub peppermint essential oil on his temples and just behind his ears to help with nausea. He liked that. Then I would set my phone alarm for another thirty minutes and either sit in the sunroom or on the porch. I often sat in our darkened bedroom watching over him for a little while, but I knew it was also important to seek light and the sun. Sometimes I would just stare mindlessly up into the trees. Sometimes I would pray.

Gary and I share a wonderful intellectual relationship. We love each other's humor, share a curiosity about so many things, and have many meaningful conversations. However, during his hospital stay for pancreatitis and during chemo, he rarely spoke. He felt too awful, and the nausea sapped his energy. Of course I understood and didn't talk much myself, but I was incredibly lonely. I could have reached out to so many, but I wanted *him*. Before this happened to us, I'd never considered the loneliness involved in fighting a disease like cancer. Now I realized my loneliness was yet another front in this battle. Everything was different. I missed Gary so much. For me, his silence was deafening.

In October, after four of these chemo rounds, Gary had another battery of tests to see if the tumor was responding to the chemo. Several days later, we were scheduled to see the medical oncologist for the news. So much was riding on the findings! In 55% of "pancan" patients, the cancer has already spread to other major organs before the person even has symptoms. In an additional 30% of patients, although the cancer hasn't spread, the tumor is considered inoperable because it is located too close to a major vein. Altogether,

Chapter 5 – #Godhears

pancreatic cancer is considered inoperable 85% of the time. That's why pancreatic cancer is considered a "silent killer." Gary's sister flew in from Maryland to go to the afternoon appointment with us. The closer it got to the appointment time, the more anxious we became. All three of us were a bundle of nerves. Gary paced and vomited from the stress. His sister and I talked some, but mostly we sat quietly, deep in our own thoughts. I hugged my border collies like never before.

As luck would have it, the oncologist was running behind that day, but his news was worth the wait. The chemo had been effective, and the CT scan showed that the tumor had shrunk by about half – one of the greatest responses this oncologist had ever seen! He told us we would need to come back the following day to see Dr. Awesome and get his opinion regarding whether the tumor had been reduced enough that it could be removed now. We were shocked! We had been told two months earlier that shrinking the tumor enough to remove it would likely take eight or more rounds of chemo. Gary, his sister, and I sat in that exam room and just stared at each other. We couldn't believe it yet.

Gary's sister did that day's entry to the private social media group. The date was October 31st:

"Happy tears in this car on the way home from the doctor visit. Preliminary report is the tumor is SHRINKING, and Gary is kicking this cancer to the curb. The cancer count in his blood has dropped dramatically. Follow up visit tomorrow with the surgeon to talk about how much more chemo he needs before surgery but he is definitely trending in the right direction. In Gary's heartfelt words to Julie upon hearing the news, "You may have to put up with me for a few more decades."

Oh, God. Yes! Please, please, please YES!

Chapter 5 – #Godhears

The next day's visit with Dr. Awesome brought even more good news. He believed the tumor had responded enough that he could get it all during surgery and that we shouldn't wait. He thought the tumor had deadened enough around the edges and had pulled away from that major vein enough for him to remove the entire tumor.

To this, Gary asked, "If the chemo is working, doesn't it make sense to keep doing the chemo to make even MORE progress? To increase your chances of being able to get the whole tumor?"

"Excellent question," Dr. Awesome responded. "There is some chance that this tumor is still shedding cells that will try to colonize in other places. Also, the tumor could begin to develop resistance to the chemo. There's no denying this tumor has responded to the chemo you've had so far. This is the time to strike." I couldn't help but notice the battle imagery again.

Dr. Awesome also explained the surgery again and described it, the Whipple Procedure, as "the most complicated surgery in all of surgery."

"What?" I recall thinking. "Isn't a heart transplant or something more complicated than this?"

No. Apparently not. This is a very complicated surgery given how deeply the pancreas is embedded in the body. Dr. Awesome would have to "rewire" Gary's entire digestive system and re-connect it to what was left of his pancreas. Gary's body would have to learn how to digest food in this new system, so holding down food after this surgery would be an incredible challenge. Dr. Awesome told Gary he would lose another 20 or 25 pounds. Gary was already so thin! I couldn't imagine him losing another 25 pounds. And if the remaining part of the pancreas didn't produce enough

Chapter 5 – #Godhears

insulin, Gary would also become a diabetic. Dr. Awesome added that the procedure is pretty risky and that some patients die on the table. He reassured us by saying that his stats are far better than the national average, but it was startling to hear this just the same.

That night in bed, Gary and I talked about how we believed God had interceded for us yet again. The tumor had responded in "only" four treatments instead of the estimated 8-12, and Dr. Awesome believed it was now possible to get it all. Could these be miracles? We weren't sure. We certainly believe God is in control, that He loves his children, that He opens and closes doors, and that He may sometimes intervene supernaturally. Whether these were miracles or not, all of it was big news! Not only was the tumor now considered operable, Gary would go into this serious surgery stronger than if he'd had more chemo treatments. While we were overjoyed with this news, it was also sobering to think about surgery. Once again, the ground had shifted beneath our feet. We'd been told that <u>IF</u> the surgery could happen, it probably wouldn't happen until after Christmas. Things were happening fast again. This serious, serious surgery was right around the corner.

Could we really ask God for yet another miracle? This would be a big one.

Gary's surgery was scheduled for Monday, November 21st. During this time, I was doing many things to PRO-act. I was deliberately choosing to have hope and faith every day, but there were days that I faltered. I worried that the same man couldn't receive yet another miracle. I worried that we'd already used up our allotment. That I shouldn't be asking for more. Gary and I had talked so often about how God isn't some big vending machine in the sky… how you can't put in a certain amount of prayers or good works in exchange for

Chapter 5 – #Godhears

what you want. Gary had also taught me that while God's Word teaches us to pray boldly for things, prayer also helps us prepare our hearts to accept God's plan for our lives – whatever the outcome. How often I'd heard Gary say during this battle, "Regardless of how this turns out, my life's purpose doesn't change. My purpose is to bring glory to God."

"Oh, God…" I would pray. I couldn't help myself. "Please let Gary live! Please let Dr. Awesome get the whole tumor! Please let this surgery be successful! Please, God! Please let Gary live!" I usually prayed these prayers the most at night, looking up at the star-filled sky while outside with my dogs for their potty break. I would stare at the sky and beg God to hear me. Tears always fell. I knew the whole vending machine thing, but I begged a lot anyway. I marveled countless times at Gary's strength, faith, and conviction. His faith was unflappable. Mine, though… mine faltered at times. What helped me was to pray, choose, and do.

Choosing Hope ~ Then & Now

Gary survived the surgery and is doing remarkably well. I call him my "walking miracle," and indeed everyone at the chemo centers love to see him coming. He's a success story – at least for now – in a place where sickness and death often prevails. It took Gary several months to learn how to eat again, but now he eats well and has gained his weight back. He also endured six more months of post-op chemotherapy. While this had some hard side effects, he was only on two drugs instead of three. These were a little easier on his system. As of this writing, he's still recovering from chemo, but he's had his first round of clear CT scans and bloodwork. He'll have this elaborate testing every three months for

Chapter 5 – #Godhears

several years. If he stays cancer free for five years, he'll earn the "I Beat Pancreatic Cancer" t-shirt.

If he can get to that point, we'll probably be at Miracle #20. Or more. We still play offense on things we can control: our eating habits, our rest and exercise, our prayer life, practicing gratitude even for small things, and most importantly, our decision to choose hope and faith over fear and doubt.

So many people helped us during this frightening, uncertain time in our lives. My colleagues carried my weight at work, and the ladies in Gary's office carried his weight. Our family and friends did countless practical things like mow our lawn, watch our dogs, contribute to gift cards, and send bright cards in the mail. Many people prayed every day for us and kept us on their church's or home group's prayer list for months. My sister stacked my freezer with healthy meals. Mom fasted and prayed. Gary's parents and sisters spent Christmas with us since we couldn't travel. The lady in my employer's benefits office was compassionate, helpful, and responded to all my questions immediately. Then there's a lady (whose name I never even knew) at the hospital in Dallas who made me a veggie omelet one morning and then came around from behind the stove to hug and hug me, all the while praying in my ear while I sobbed. Yet, another lady at this same cafeteria (whose name I also never even knew) did the same thing several months later, again while I sobbed. Nurses and doctors gave us exceptional care and answered all of our questions. Nurses on the chemo hotline gently and patiently listened to my frantic questions about side effects. Dr. Awesome and his staff…. Well, the list is endless. We'll never be able to repay these kindnesses, but we promised to pay them forward. This writing is one attempt to do that and why I have included more than just the events as they happened. Included below are specific, purposeful things I

Chapter 5 – #Godhears

did – and that Gary did, too – to win the game against pancreatic cancer. By the time you read this, know that I've been praying my words will bless and help you.

1. If I've learned anything in all of this, it's that HOPE isn't an emotion – it's a mindset. Hope by itself isn't necessarily a strategy either, but out of a hopeful mindset can come your life-giving strategy. Your action plan. Your battle plan. The various things you can actually *do* to fight feelings of anger, despair, paralyzing fear, or bitterness in the face of a challenging situation. I know it likely sounds impossible or "Pollyanna" given the situation you might be facing, but I strongly believe that if you can decide to choose hope, you must then DO things that help you stay in this hopeful mindset. You must first CHOOSE and then DO.

   How do I know this with such certainty? Because I've lived it. In my case, paralyzing fear was the biggest threat to my emotional well-being as Gary's wife and primary caregiver. The numbers for pancreatic cancer are grim, and on top of that, he was so, so sick at times. I was deeply afraid Gary would die, and I would get gripped by fear and uncertainty regarding how I would handle things in that reality. I simply couldn't imagine losing him, but I knew that was a very real possibility. It was (and still is) such a weird mix of emotion. Gary and I know for certain that he will go to heaven if he loses this battle. We both believe that Jesus died for our sins and prepared a place for us there, so we aren't afraid of what comes after life on this earth. It's so liberating and wonderful to have this certainty about going to

Chapter 5 – #Godhears

heaven! It's why Gary's faith was so unshakable even during the hardest days. So, you see? Death isn't really the problem. The problem for me... and what paralyzes me with fear if I let it... is life without my best friend and soul mate.

I'm still learning that sometimes choosing hope has to be daily and purposeful. Gary and I had decided that very first night that we would have faith in God's perfect plan and that we would fight. That was our CHOICE. I knew that intellectually, but at first, I didn't know how to actually believe it. That's when I began realizing that this choice needed to turn into an action of some kind – our DO – which would help our decision stick. For me, it started when a doctor told me not to Google pancreatic cancer. But, I'm a reader. It's what I do when the ground gives way beneath my feet, so to not read anything at all would have fed my fear. It would have made me feel even more powerless and vulnerable. Instead, I chose to read about how to FIGHT cancer – not about how cancer kills. I began reading about foods that can help a body fight cancer and then shared some of this information with Gary.

The real gift here is that researching something positive – in my case, the health benefits of eating more plants, fruits, and whole grains – created positivity. Instead of reading about cancer, tumors, and death, I was reading about LIFE! This shift to positivity made a tremendous impact on our approach to such a life-threatening, scary diagnosis.

I can "toil and spin" better than anyone, but God's Word tells us not to worry. Easier said than done, though, right? For me, reading how others fought

Chapter 5 – #Godhears

cancer through their diet and learning how to make healthy, flavorful recipes gave me something to DO. It engaged my brain and was a productive outlet for my nervous energy. It was a way to PRO-act. So much of the cancer journey and chemo's side effects make you feel powerless, like a victim, like all you can do is RE-act. Certainly, Gary and I did have to react to side effects and what he could or couldn't eat, but it helped our emotional head game tremendously to engage in things that were PRO-active. This was a game-changer for us. Play defense when necessary, but also play offense.

I also dumped out several of my flower pots and planted kale and cilantro. "Kale?" you might be thinking. "Really? Kale? I hate kale, and spinach is a close second." Friends, that's pretty much how we felt prior to a serious cancer diagnosis. I went from not ever eating kale to growing it. I chuckle about this now, but looking back, I can see that one positive action led to another. For example, our neighbor gave me a packet of kale seeds, and it felt so good that day to put my hands in rich potting soil and plant those little seeds. I loved watering the seeds and watching them grow. When the kale matured and I could add tender leaves to the smoothies I made for Gary, it felt so good! All of this "doing" was life-giving and encouraging.

And thus, began our strategy to fight back! My brother had encouraged me to "Charge ahead!" and making these choices became an integral part of our battle plan. When I fixed Gary a healthy meal or made him a delicious, spinach/kale-packed smoothie, I would often imagine those anti-oxidants

Chapter 5 – #Godhears

were little soldiers that were racing around Gary's body and punching out cancer cells! (Incidentally, you might be surprised by how much the taste of spinach and kale can be masked by blackberries, raspberries, and bananas!) Other anti-oxidants operated huge battering rams that tirelessly rammed into Gary's tumor to make it pull away from that vein. It was working! I just knew it was!

I know it's silly, but this imagery motivated me to keep trying new recipes and to figure out ways to prepare nutrient-dense meals for this man I loved so much. Actions like these gave us a way to meet cancer on the battlefield. Sometimes, I thought about the shepherd boy who became King David; while others hid in caves, David prayed and then faced Goliath head-on. For him, victory in the face of seemingly impossible odds came through fighting – not hiding.

If you're facing a disease, helping a loved one recover from a tragic accident, or facing any other kind of challenge, what can you CHOOSE and DO? I encourage you to give this idea thought and to even ask a friend to help you. What choices will help you have a positive, I'm-going-to-win-this-battle mindset? While it's tempting to feel sorry for yourself or to have a victim mentality, I strongly encourage you to fight this urge. Choose hope, faith, and positivity to improve your head game. CHOOSE and then DO.

2. Make a gratitude list. It's another action that is life-giving. In the early days of this diagnosis, one of Gary's sisters created a private social media page for

Chapter 5 – #Godhears

me to update our closest family members and friends about how Gary was doing. This was incredibly helpful in managing the communication and I especially loved being able to quickly ask for specific prayers. However, some posts were challenging to write because I had to include hard news.

One day, I spontaneously added, "Today's Gratitude List" to the end of a post. From then on, I would list between 3-5 things on many of these posts. To be honest, there were days that were so bad that I struggled to come up with anything for the list. But, in my own words that I typed on September 9th of last year: *"As for the gratitude lists I'm posting each time, I realized yesterday those are actually more for me than anyone else. This list is an accountability partner of sorts and makes me purposefully consider the day's blessings."*

3. Try to maintain your sense of humor. Laughter is good for the body in so many ways. When we laugh, endorphins are released in our brain, which can improve our overall sense of well-being and even reduce stress. And, as I'm still learning, laughing at myself is a more life-giving choice than getting angry, frustrated, or sad. An example of this is the morning I dropped my iPhone in the toilet (you know you've done it too, or have come close to it!):

"Today's Gratitude List (September 21st)
1. Sisters
2. My friend Amy
3. That my iPhone still works after dropping it in the toilet. (So... this morning - right after I got up - I was donning my bathrobe in my closet and heard the toilet running. I put my phone in the pocket of my robe and headed into the toilet

Chapter 5 – #Godhears

room. I needed to remove the back of the toilet, so I took several things off the back of the toilet to set on the floor. As I bent down to do that, my phone dropped into the toilet. YIKES! Thankfully the water was clean...... should that be considered #4 above?..... I grabbed my phone immediately, yanked off the protective cover, and dried it. Then I raced to the kitchen, jerked open a box of Gary's organic, wild rice, and submerged my phone in the rice where it stayed for several hours. Unbelievably, it seems to be working fine! I'm also grateful I had the foresight to put on my readers and just BE SURE there wasn't a small piece of rice hiding in the charging hole on the phone. There was, so I was soooooo glad I removed it before jamming the charger in there.)"

I did eventually have to replace my iPhone, which was a hassle, but I got some laughter mileage out of telling the above story. When you're in the fight of your life, try to find reasons to laugh. Be on the lookout for funny things in your everyday life. Here's another example from our first time to sign in Gary at the cancer clinic for chemo:

"September 7th

Ooops! We just learned that when you sign in on the sticker sign-in pad, the sticker STAYS at the desk so they know you're here. It doesn't go on your chest like it's a name tag. Ha! #firsttimers #sosilly."

You could also watch funny videos on YouTube, play with your dog, watch funny movies, or whatever will give you a chuckle. You could even ask several friends to send you funny things to view if you're too busy to find them yourself. Friends want to help when there's a crisis, and I bet you've got several of them who would love to do this for you.

4. Related to this, consider reducing how much you watch the news or read troubling articles on social

media if you're facing a difficult time in your life. I know there are serious things happening in our nation and in our world, but during Gary's cancer fight, I couldn't handle the negativity and anger in the news. I just couldn't think about things happening "out there" when my own house was on fire. I decided that those things would have to wait. This might greatly help your overall sense of hope and well-being, too.

5. Sit in the sun. Vitamin D is so good for the human body and is known to elevate mood. I tried to do this a little each day, even if it was chilly outside. It was often during this "sun time" that I would pray or brainstorm more things to add to my "DO" list. Vitamin D also gives you energy. This is an easy one to skip when we get busy, but try not to very often. It's important.

6. Post encouraging words or Scriptures in prominent places around your house. I began signing my posts in the private social media group with #Godhears, so my sister made banners that say "#Godhears" and "#wagehope." They were hanging in our kitchen when Gary and I arrived home from the hospital after his surgery to remove the tumor. I moved one to the sunroom, but those banners hung in these public areas in our home for months until Gary completed his post-op chemotherapy. They're now in our bedroom where they'll likely stay for years until Gary earns the right to say he beat pancreatic cancer.

Chapter 5 – #Godhears

I also put a huge, bright green post-it note eye level on our refrigerator door with two of my favorite Scriptures:

"For God has not given us a spirit of fear, but of power, and of love, and of a sound mind" (2 Timothy 1:7).

and

"God is our refuge and strength, an ever-present help in times of trouble. Therefore will not we fear, though the earth be removed, and though the mountains be carried into the midst of the sea… the Lord of Hosts is with us; the God of Jacob is our refuge…Be still and know that I am God…"

Singing songs and reading encouraging words were yet even more actions. CHOOSE and then DO. I'd chosen to believe God's word about conquering my fears, but I had to DO things to continually reinforce this belief with life-giving actions. Every time I opened the refrigerator door, these Scriptures poured into my mind if even at a subconscious level. I believe this helped me. Everyone has different verses, songs, and poems that speak to them. What are yours? If you don't want to post these publicly, at least journal them and re-read them each day.

~ Parting Thoughts ~

The slogan for pancreatic cancer awareness is "Wage Hope." This didn't mean much at first, but now I get it! With cancer, you definitely have to wage battle and wage hope. By following exactly what the doctors said, eating a plant-based diet, and exercising, we did our best not to let cancer and chemo just happen. Gary and I made a choice that first night to wage battle! With the help of so many, we continue to meet cancer on the battlefield. And we are fighting to WIN.

God may not be parting the Red Sea anymore, but during the past year, I've had a front-row seat to the many miracles he's STILL doing in our lives. Yes, God hears. Take heart, my friends! God definitely hears.

#Godhears

#Wagehope

#TeamLeslie

And now ... #TeamYou.

About the Author – Julie Leslie

Julie Martin Leslie founded *In Your Element Coaching & Consulting* after resigning from her job to help her husband Gary battle pancreatic cancer. Prior to this resignation, Julie worked in public education for 21 years. She led the gifted and talented department for seven years in a large school district north of Dallas and received a state leadership award for this work in 2015. Julie taught high school for fourteen years prior to that. After recent months spent learning more about hospitals, cancer, and chemotherapy than she ever wanted to know, Julie believes God is calling her to share specific strategies that help her choose hope during the scariest season of her life.

Julie earned her undergraduate degree from Penn State, her master's degree from Texas A&M-Commerce, and hopes to finish her doctorate in leadership at Dallas Baptist University. She resides in Texas with her husband, step-son, and two border collies. She would love to add your hope ideas to her list or to work with your group, either in person or virtually. Julie has helped many teens discover their "element" related to choosing a college and major. She also facilitates insightful, fun, and often life-changing mastermind

Chapter 5 – #Godhears

groups about leadership, effective communication, learning from failure, and personal growth.

Julie invites you to visit her website at www.InYourElement.info and to contact her!

Chapter 5 – #Godhears

Chapter 5 – #Godhears

Chapter 6

The Gift of Blessing Others
By Mark Brown

Take a moment to recall the most entertaining and educational story you've read or heard so far in your life. Do you have it firmly affixed in your memory right now? What was it about that story that kept you reading or listening to it? Did you read it for entertainment, or education, or both?

As you read this chapter, you might learn a few things that you can apply in your life that will help you to enjoy the journey of life as you know it.

Hello, my name is Mark Edward Brown. Allow me to share my life story with you as you look over my shoulder and see a perspective of a professional who is blessed in his mission of helping men and women all over the world go from down and out, to loving life.

My hope is that you will learn insights and gain wisdom that have taken me a lifetime to learn. I am happy to share them with you because I want you to not only enjoy this story, I want you to put its lessons into practice in your life so you can live at a level of clarity, joy, and fulfillment that is aligned with God's plan. Remove the current distractions that are

Chapter 6 – The Gift of Blessing Others

surrounding you (cell phone, TV, background noise) and engage your full concentration, let's get started…

I was born in the early 1970's to a man and woman who, at the time, were happily married and living in a rural farming town in the mid-western United States of America. The first few years of life, to my recollection, were rather uneventful, except for one particular occurrence that is still as fresh in my memory as if it was yesterday. I am the oldest of three children and the only boy in the family, so being my sisters' older brother and the "man" around the house when my Dad was gone, I had a lot on my shoulders.

My younger sister and I were in my Dad's pick-up on a Saturday morning and we were going to the bakery to get some rolls and doughnuts for breakfast. Our Dad forgot something in the apartment we were living in, so he had gone back in the building to get whatever it was that he had forgotten. I had slid over into the driver's position behind the wheel of the pick-up and was pretending to drive, just like I had seen my Dad do on many occasions before. My little sister was sliding off the seat next to me and right as her feet were about to touch down on the floor of the vehicle, she reached out to steady herself. What she grabbed as she was steadying herself was the gearshift, which in those days was located on the right-hand side of the steering column.

When she grabbed the gearshift, she dislodged the vehicle from "Park" to "Neutral." As the pickup began to creep forward, my short life flashed before my eyes. My sister was looking up at me and the last thing that went through my mind was, *How do I stop this vehicle from rolling forward and crashing through the basement apartment right in front of us. The pickup used*

Chapter 6 – The Gift of Blessing Others

to be parked and now it's slowly rolling forward towards one of the basement apartment units. I did not cry. I calmly slid straight down between the seat and steering wheel and with both feet stood directly on the brake. Right as the vehicle came to a stop, my sister hopped back up on the seat and sat down calmly like nothing had happened.

I turned my head to the right and twisted my torso to look at her and make sure she was all right. The pickup had come to a stop, and I did not have a view of the outside anymore because I wasn't a very tall kid. Just then, I heard my Dad exclaim in a loud and surprised voice, "What in the world is going on here?" The driver's side door opened and my Dad's eyes were wide with wonder, surprise, and what I thought was anger. Seeing so much emotion on my Dad's face and hearing his loud booming voice, caused me to cry because I became scared and I thought I was in BIG trouble.

He reached into the pickup and immediately put the vehicle in park. He gently reached down and picked me up from between the seat and steering wheel. He sat me down on the seat between himself and my little sister and then backed the pickup up about 4 feet. He then turned the vehicle off and asked, "Kids, what happened? Mark, what were you doing?" I told him that we were playing and pretending like we were driving around and then the pickup started to move and I knew I had to stop it before it crashed into the apartment building. I did not tell him that my little sister had slipped the vehicle out of park and into neutral.

My Dad said, "You and your sister could have been hurt very badly, what you did was very impressive – you're my hero, little man!" We then proceeded to drive to the bakery and I

Chapter 6 – The Gift of Blessing Others

got to pick out as many of my favorite doughnuts as I wanted that day. It all happened so fast, yet when the critical moment occurred where life and death hung in the balance, everything slowed down and there was a calm, confidence knowing precisely what to do and that it must be done immediately. Looking back, I feel that situation was clearly one point in time that God's protective power firmly empowered me to act in a manner far exceeding what is typical of a child who normally would be frozen with fear or unknowing of the circumstances going on around him or her. This was the first time that the saying, "Let go and let God" was fully experienced in my life. It was a blessing to feel the Holy Spirit alive in me, and it would not be the last time as you will continue to read on and learn what happens next.

Fast forward a few years after that event and as a young boy, I spent time with my grandparents, aunts, and uncles learning to crawl, walk, run, say the alphabet, read, write, and do arithmetic. I would spend summers with my cousins, who were also my best friends, and we would play outside from dusk 'til dawn, only going indoors to have lunch and dinner, to then do it all again the next day.

Growing up in the mid-western United States required using your imagination. We were always creating adventures, pretending we were cowboys out riding the range like the Lone Ranger, playing cops and robbers, and fighting epic battles with our stick guns in an imaginary war zone in a faraway land.

On any given day during the summer, my cousin and I would wake up late after staying up late into the night listening to

Chapter 6 – The Gift of Blessing Others

the radio, playing board games like Monopoly, and drinking soda pop, even though we knew we weren't supposed to. Yes indeed, we were truly rebellious, and on one particular day, a very memorable event occurred. We were trudging through a back alley that ran parallel to the main street in the small country town my cousin lived in when we heard a noise and were compelled to investigate its origins.

Most of the towns that my cousins lived in and that I grew up in only had one "main" street; they weren't very big and if I had to guess, the population ranged from just under 1,000 to 3,500 occupants at the most. I was so country that my parents had me wearing cowboy boots long into my elementary school days. I've got pictures of me in western shirts and a cowboy hat to boot.

Back to the story, my cousin and I happened upon an enormous beast like we had never seen before in our young lives. This animal was gigantic in its short yet stocky frame and it made shrieking sounds that we could not describe and had never heard before. When we first heard its shrill screams of desperation and fright, we were instantly in investigation mode. Our eyes met, wide with curiosity, and we began sneaking toward the wooden fenced-in area that kept this beast penned up and away from prying eyes.

This was a warm summer morning, and the wailing beast that was squealing and slamming into the boards that kept this hulking animal penned in captivated our attention. As we crept closer, we had no idea what to expect, and we could hear water splashing on the cement of the animal pen as if someone was purposely calming the animal or making it mad. We found a sturdy wooden box that was nearby and

Chapter 6 – The Gift of Blessing Others

grabbed the top of the fence to climb up and peek over to see what was causing all of the noise that we had heard on the other side of the fence.

We looked down into the clearing and saw the biggest, most plump, loud hog that we had ever seen in our lives. Eyeing the stream of water, there was a man who was purposefully spraying the huge pig with water. Seeing us with our eyes wide with wonder the man said, "What are you boys doing today?" We were frozen with anxiety and excitement and didn't know what to do or say. What we had just discovered was the back of the local meat market and grocery store.

My cousin and I spent the entire morning and part of the afternoon fascinated by what we had happened upon and asked the butcher countless questions. Many years ago, small-town butchers processed their animals at their stores where the meat was prepared and sold. I think he was surprised that we were so curious about the how, what, and why of the butchering process. Just as the animal was put out of its misery and the butcher was about to begin the actual business of preparing it for processing, my Dad found us and said that several of my uncles, aunts, and cousins had been looking for us because we had missed lunch, which was something we had never done before. We lost track of time, but the store owner vouched for our whereabouts and urged my Dad not to punish us because we were behaving well and he enjoyed educating us about his trade. I thought back to this event many times in the following weeks, and one of the key lessons I learned was that I wanted to be of service to people when I became an adult. Some people are called to do hard jobs that others consider brutal, yet they are necessary in order for life to carry on.

Chapter 6 – The Gift of Blessing Others

The next event in my young life that I recall was so unexpected and traumatic that it shook me to the core of my being and forged an internal, emotional resilience that has served me well throughout my childhood, teen years, and into adulthood. I do not remember exactly who told my younger sisters and me; it was either my Mom or Dad. When they told us that they would no longer be living together, our world was turned upside down.

There was a brief period of separation between my parents before we were told that our Mom and Dad were getting a divorce. This was so incomprehensible. We never saw it coming. I remember going numb in my body and mind. My parents had been married for at least ten years, perhaps longer.

I became devious and delinquent. I no longer trusted adults, mainly because the two that I loved the most in my life stopped loving each other. I grew bitter and began hanging out with other troubled kids who were my age or just slightly older. I thought that maybe they would be able to share some ideas about why bad things happen to good kids and they might know how to deal with the heartache, guilt, and a bunch of other feelings that kids are not emotionally equipped to deal with.

My experience growing up as a teen was troubled, to say the least. I made no effort to make or keep friends because I was so confused. I wasn't an outright bad boy or punk; I was, however, a sneaky, sarcastic, and a manipulative delinquent. I'm going to outline how I turned my life around in a moment, but for now, it's important to know that my parents had their own drama to worry about and my teachers were

Chapter 6 – The Gift of Blessing Others

not very aware of the emotional baggage that I was wrestling with as I grew into a young adult.

I was spiritually empty, or so I thought, and even though I knew the Lord was there for me, I was angry and wanted nothing to do with religion or a Savior. My Mom was the one who raised her voice frequently like Mom's do and told me to shape up. My Dad was the one who would ground me and a Step-Dad tried to get me on the right track. I was not given any "life-changing" advice that turned it all around for me, though. I was yelled at enough to learn how to "tune out" anyone that raised their voice or stuck their finger in my direction.

My redemption began as I turned inward to attempt to sort out my feelings. Physical exercise became my primary coping mechanism. Running was the main way that I dealt with stress, anger, hostility, and a myriad of other emotions that I could barely control in front of other people.

Periodically, we lived in the country and I would run through the fields. When we lived in a town or city and I had a bicycle, I would peddle as hard as I could wherever I went. Once, when my bike was stolen, I reverted to running again, so you can imagine that my ability to jog or run was virtually effortless at this point. There was no slowing down for me. If I could help it, I would not jog. It was not until later in high school when I was on the track or cross-country team; I realized that sometimes it was necessary to pace oneself so that victory could be achieved.

One remarkable adult that did make quite a difference in my life was my martial arts instructor. I began the study of self-defense and meditation in Moo Duk Kwon, Karate, and

Chapter 6 – The Gift of Blessing Others

eventually Tae Kwon Do; I did not earn the degree of black belt until much later in life.

Additionally, I began reading with a thirst for knowledge that is hard to explain. Thanks to an English teacher and librarian who introduced me to the most captivating, science fiction novels a kid would ever want to read. I found a way to escape reality temporarily and learn anything my imagination would allow. I also enjoyed learning and reading about the history of the USA. History was always an enjoyable subject and I remember learning about it and the people. This played a pivotal role in forming the foundation of my patriotism and love for my country and its people.

I also became quite an entrepreneur as I learned to use successful communication to reason, negotiate, and sell services and products to other people. During the cold winter months, I would shovel snow from driveways and sidewalks. One technique that I used to maximize my earnings was to ask what that person felt my time was worth to them. I would remind them that I freed up time for them and removed a hazardous situation simultaneously. This allowed me to maximize my earnings and at the same time made my clients feel good that they were financially helping a kid in need.

In the summertime, I would mow lawns and I used the same sales and earning technique to gain the most money I could. I sold boxes of greeting cards and even applied my talent as a young magician. All of this was building a unique foundation within me that later in life I would be able to identify and use in order to help and bless other people.

Chapter 6 – The Gift of Blessing Others

As I was rounding a corner in my life from a sad point to a more industrious and optimistic outlook, there was still one area of it all that just did not resonate with my being. Due to my less than stellar grades throughout junior high and high school, plus a lack of interest in farm-related jobs, I knew that I had to do something to change the turbulent trajectory that my life was on. That day came for me one afternoon in High School. A recruiter from my state's National Guard spoke with the boys in my class, and with the assistance of the guidance counselor, I made an appointment for him to meet with my Mom and Step-Dad.

I was eager to become an army soldier because there were two things that I did when playing as a kid. I would always play cops and robbers or army. I do not know why I never pretended to be a marine or sailor, and flying never interested me, so the air force was out of the question. With the help of the recruiter and my negotiating skills, my parents agreed to allow me to go to "boot camp" the summer between my junior and senior year of high school. The following year after I graduated, I attended training for a Military Occupational Specialty (M.O.S.).

Enlisting in any branch of the military is an experience no one forgets, there is more paperwork than any other transaction I have done in my life. Buying a house or car has nothing on the number of signatures I signed as my parents and I began my journey in the Army.

I attended basic training at Fort Leonard Wood, Missouri in the summer of 1989. That summer, the training I experienced and the young man those drill sergeants turned me into was the beginning of my "new start." I left the lazy,

Chapter 6 – The Gift of Blessing Others

prideful, and egotistical kid from my past behind as I poured my full attention and intention into becoming a soldier. I knew that I had a lot of ground to gain back from those years that I was adrift and not too serious about my future.

There are countless accounts of how United States Army Drill Sergeants turn young men and women into respectful adults capable of utilizing discipline, their minds, and bodies to do amazing things. I began re-attending Church services on Sundays and felt a renewed sense of comfort and joy. As a result of these rapid changes, I formulated three goals for my final year of high school:

1) Improve my grades, graduate, and potentially attend college later if I chose to.
2) Be a better friend, person, and athlete.
3) Get a job so that I could have my own money and buy a car.

With my life moving in the right direction, I graduated from high school, then completed Nuclear, Chemical, and Biological Weapons Specialist training at Fort McClellan, Alabama. As a young adult, I worked, attended three semesters of college, and served in the Army National Guard. However, there was still something that I felt was lacking in my young life and two years after having a taste of structure, discipline, pride, and patriotism, I transferred out of the National Guard and into active duty in the United States Army.

I served for 25 years beginning as an enlisted man, earning a commission, commanding soldiers, and finally retiring at the rank of Major. I will tell you that at any given time, all the men and women who serve our nation make up

Chapter 6 – The Gift of Blessing Others

approximately one percent of our nation's entire population. I'm proud to be one of those who served and protected the rights and way of life of all men, women, and children in the United States of America. I use every ounce of experience learned, both good and bad, to help men and women around the world be the best that they can be in their pursuit of achieving personal and business success.

There are many accounts of Biblical business principles and the success that follows from living and putting into practice the lessons that are taught by clergy and Sunday school teachers. It amazes me when I see or hear of a new "business discovery" or "self-improvement" technique because I can track back their concepts or philosophies to teachings that come from the Bible. One example is being blessed to recognize when the Holy Spirit is guiding you through a life lesson. Some folks learn through a combination of trial and error while others learn from other people's examples and advice. Take a lesson from the good book and listen to the voice of the Lord. Having coaches and mentors is important. However, it's even more important that person be sanctified, biblically balanced, and have the true heart of a servant.

There is no single road to success; there are many paths that one can take to arrive at the destination of the calling on one's life. The one undeniable commonality that I can attribute my success to is trusting the Lord to network and associate with the right people. It's a proven fact that the right people can help you get to where you want to go in life.

I've been blessed with a gift of being able to show people how to become self-leaders, achievers, happy, healthy, and

Chapter 6 – The Gift of Blessing Others

wealthy in every way that they want and deserve. Are you one of them? Have you tried before, but fallen short of your goal? It's much easier to start anew when you have accountability and a proven process and teacher to assist you.

When you have someone in your corner who has been there and done that, it's often the advantage that gets you what you want versus those who decided to go at it alone and not identify the missing ingredient. That one component, characteristic, or aspect that they didn't even know they were missing because they didn't have a coach, mentor, or teacher to tell them or show them what they were missing or where they were going wrong.

I know that you have a unique gift that you were blessed with and my calling in life is to help those who have lost sight of that gift. It's in every person who is born and who believes in the Lord. I'm proof that one can be lost, found, and triumph beyond what was imagined in a way that brings blessing forth into the world and enriches life.

You've just read several examples of how God touches the lives of people and blesses them in various ways. The blessing that I received is helping other people find their life's calling. If you think you do not have "a calling" or that you have been blessed, simply re-read this chapter and compare it to your own life. I know you will be able to see similar situations where you have been blessed and then you will know that there is proof in your life of blessings received.

Thank you for investing your time into learning about my story and mission in life. My goal was to entertain, inform, and educate you. I look forward to meeting you and getting to know you better in the future. I know I will not meet everyone who reads this chapter so I will leave you with my slogan and mission statement:

Benefiting Billions / -- Motivating Millions / -- Training Thousands / -- Helping Hundreds and showing Seekers of Success "How-To" transform their lives and businesses one person at a time!

Chapter 6 – The Gift of Blessing Others

About the Author – Mark Brown

Speaker, Trainer, & Author, Mark Edward Brown's mission in life is to help people succeed in life and business. His calling in life is coaching people who want to improve their life right now. Mark specializes in Personal Power, Successful Communication, and Leadership.

Mark works with people from all over the world. He shows people how to harness their own personal power. Once that is achieved, effective communication is a key component of his program. After personal power and successful communication are utilized, leadership is infused and a synergy becomes available for people who want to take their lives to the next level of achievement or success.

Husband, Father, Son, Friend, and Military Veteran he has lived a life rich in experiences that taught lessons which improved his ability to teach, coach, and mentor. His service-based living style and high-level of determination and discipline fuel his thirst for sharing with people how to weather the storms of life's adversity.

Helping people to discover their own unique personal power is one of the ways he finds joy in life. Mark also helps people share their gifts through successful communication and leadership.

Chapter 6 – The Gift of Blessing Others

We all communicate yet, the ability to use successful communication and leadership improves the enjoyment factor of everyday living.

www.MarkEdwardBrown.com

www.Facebook.com/MarkEdwardBrown

www.Linkedin.com/in/markedwardbrown

https://plus.google.com/u/0/104863561911270348658

Twitter: @MarkEdwardBrown

Chapter 6 – The Gift of Blessing Others

Chapter 7 – Are You Fully Equipped?

Chapter 7

Are You Fully Equipped?
By Mike Rodriguez

Most people don't think about the beginning of their life this way, but on the day that you were born, it was just you and God. Yes, your mother was there as a vessel to give birth and a doctor was there as a resource, but it was only you and God when the journey of your life started. God gave you everything you need to succeed in this world. I'll prove it as you walk through this with me:

What clothing were you born wearing? None.

What material possessions did you have when you were born? None.

In fact, when you were born, you didn't have anything except God. It was only you and Him and what He equipped you with for your life. He provided you with eyes to see, ears to hear and a nose and lungs to breathe. You probably have two arms, two hands and ten fingers to grasp, two legs to walk and two feet to stand. God gave you a mouth to talk and eat, a digestive system, a reproductive system, an immune system, a heart to keep you alive and even complex brain tissue for you to think, feel and be. He gave you all of your personal resources, for His purposes for YOUR life.

Know that God doesn't make mistakes.

God gave you everything you need to succeed in this world. If you don't or didn't have any of the mentioned body parts, then that is a part of His plan for your life as well. You were born prepared for His plans for your life. It is a truth that most of us never really think about because we tend to mess things up. We do this by adding negative things to our lives that He never gave us or even intended for us to have. We add these things, then we falsely define them as a part of who we are.

We are born perfect in God's eyes, fully prepared to succeed, but along the way, we lose sight of whose we are and what we're capable of achieving through trusting in Him. Life happens to us and we start engaging in bad or unhealthy things. We might begin to abuse alcohol or drugs. We might start getting angry, depressed, or create unhealthy addictions, thoughts or actions. Sometimes we completely redefine who we think we are, due to the confusion and deception in this world. However, God's message is very clear: He has already equipped you for His purpose. You just need to trust in Him, accept Him and accept who He created you to be.

When you were born, do you remember that tag made of flesh attached to your side? You know, the one that said, "addict," "depressed," "anger issues," "fearful," "worried," "confused" or something else that was negative?

Chapter 7 – Are You Fully Equipped?

No, you say? You don't remember having that or even being born with an extra flesh tag with a negative description of yourself? Of course not, because it wasn't there.

The reason it wasn't there, is because God never put it there!

This is the part where you might say, but Mike, I do have a defining negative characteristic and it is a part of me, but I've always been that way! This is where I tell you that you are wrong. God never gave you any negative defining characteristics. That was all your doing.

Living in a world dominated by sin, causes us to sin. Sometimes, we can sin so much and for so long that we can get confused and accept the sin as our own identity. We can confuse what we DO, as who we are. I challenge you to accept and believe that the things you DO, really aren't who you are. I'm not talking about shirking responsibility for your actions, I am talking about separating what God made you to be, versus what you have added to your life through what you DO. If you are doing things you shouldn't be doing, stop doing them! Once you stop doing those things, you will remove from your life what you brought in or introduced. God never intended those things to be there in the first place.

Sometimes, we do negative and sinful things for so long that we can cover ourselves in those things, hiding who we truly are. When diamonds are mined from the earth, the seekers can be deceived as they sort through thick chunks of carbon. However, if they can keep their eyes on the prize, not on the nasty carbon, the seekers can and usually will find the brilliant gems inside, covered by the years of darkness. It can be difficult to sort through thick layers of dark decay.

Chapter 7 – Are You Fully Equipped?

It requires great work to remove the layers of carbon to reveal the brilliance of the beautiful diamond inside.

Our lives with Christ are similar to mining diamonds.

God has given us His brilliant, shining light to be found inside. The challenge is that some of us have hidden the brilliant light within, by covering ourselves with layers of dark carbon, represented by years of sinful nature, negative actions, and habits. Some of us have been sinning for so long that we have falsely accepted the layers of carbon as a part of who we are. When we do this, we allow the layers of darkness to prevent God's brilliant light within us from shining to the rest of the world.

The great news is that although you may not feel like you can remove the years of negativity or darkness that you may be trapped in, God loves you and He can! He makes all things new! He can help you remove the years of negative and sinful things that have been hiding His light inside of you if you only trust in Him!

Yes, you and God started your life journey and it will be just you and God who will end your life journey together, if you know Him. Will you be prepared to give an account of what you did according to His plans for your life?

You can be prepared right now.

Here is how:

The Bible says that the only way to know God is through Jesus. In fact, Jesus said, "I am the way, the truth, and the life. No one can come to the Father except through me." John 14: 6.

Chapter 7 – Are You Fully Equipped?

This means that by asking Jesus into your life, you can know God. In your own words, pray and repent of your sins and confess that you believe Jesus died for your sins on the cross. Acknowledge Jesus Christ as your Lord and Savior and ask Him into your heart.

If you said this prayer on your own free will right now, then congratulations, you have been saved and you are fully equipped! Praise God.

However, you need to continue to do your part and live your life in a way that honors God, by trusting in Him.

Now go forth and make your life exceptional!

- Mike Rodriguez

www.MikeRodriguezInternational.com

Chapter 7 – Are You Fully Equipped?

EPILOGUE

Throughout my life, I have always felt a bigger and better purpose for my life, but I have not always been in pursuit of it, mostly because I have been my own biggest obstacle. I was often distracted by my current comfort zones through my current routines. They kept me from stepping into my full potential and kept me as a prisoner to mediocrity. I knew that I wanted to pursue God's plan for my life, I just wasn't focused enough to see it or empowered enough to take action.

After years of very strong feelings that God had something better for me, I only took action to start changing my life, when I chose to have faith and start trusting in God's plan for me. I knew this was the only way to make bigger things happen.

Through His grace, I am a new man. I understand my purpose and I am full of life. I can see Him clearly, and I am stronger than ever.

With regard to success, I have always felt that my purpose was to help others through the gift of speaking. I have always dreamed of becoming a motivational/inspirational speaker, and even a pastor, but for the largest part of my life, I only considered this a dream.

Who was I to become these things?

What credentials or gifts did I have?

These were negative thoughts that I burdened myself with.

So, who am I?

I am a son of our King.

I know Him and He knows me.

Today, all because of Him, and through my obedience to decide, take action and have faith, I am living my life's dream. I am pursuing my life's goal, and most importantly, my life's purpose to help others build their lives all for the glory of God.

Believe in God, trust in Him and His plan for your life. Have faith and take action. You too can realize your bigger purpose as the son or daughter of the same King!

Now Go Forth and Make YOUR Life Exceptional!

- **Mike Rodriguez**

About Mike Rodriguez

Mike Rodriguez is CEO of Mike Rodriguez International, LLC, a professional speaking, training and global ministry organization. Besides being a Best-Selling author, he is an international motivator and a leadership and people expert. Mike and his wife Bonnie also own a publishing company and they still manage to spend quality time with their five daughters, all while Mike is studying for his master's degree at Dallas Theological Seminary and then pursuing his MDiv at SWBTS. Mike is a former showcase speaker with the original Zig Ziglar Corporation and was selected as their key speaker for the 2015 Ziglar U.S. Tour.

Mike delivers performance-based seminars and trainings and has authored several books which have been promoted by Barnes & Noble. He has been featured on CBS, U.S. News & World Report, Success Magazine and he has lectured at Baylor University, UNT and K-State Research. His clients include names like Hilton, McDonald's Corporation, the Federal Government and many more. As a people expert, Mike has trained thousands around the world.

Everyone faces challenges; Mike believes that through faith and action, you can overcome the challenges in your life to attain your goals and become who God has called you to be.

Mike has been happily married since 1991 to Bonnie, the love of his life and together they have five beautiful daughters. He believes if you have the right attitude and the right faith, you can have the right kind of success, regardless of the type of industry that you are in.

Trusting in Him – Stories That Inspire

Trusting in Him – Stories That Inspire

As a world-renowned speaker,
Mike has experience working with people
from all walks of life.

You can schedule Mike Rodriguez
to speak, inspire or train at your next event.
Go to:
www.MikeRodriguezInternational.com

Other books available by Mike Rodriguez:

Finding Your WHY

8 Keys to Exceptional Selling

Break Your Routines to Fix Your Life

Lion Leadership

Think BIG Motivational Quotes

The Power of Breaking Routines
(Audio Course from Nightingale Conant)

Walking with Faith

A Bigger Purpose

Trusting in Him – Stories That Inspire

Trusting in Him – Stories That Inspire

Trusting in Him – Stories That Inspire

Trusting in Him – Stories That Inspire

Disclaimer & Copyright Information

Some of the events, locales, and conversations have been recreated from memories. In order to maintain their anonymity, in some instances, the names of individuals and places have been changed. As such, some identifying characteristics and details may have changed.

Although the authors and publishers have made every effort to ensure that the information in this book was correct at press time, the authors and publishers do not assume and hereby disclaim any liability to any party for any loss, damage, or disruption caused by errors or omissions, whether such errors or omissions result from negligence, accident, or any other cause. Each author is responsible for the content of each story.

All quotes, unless otherwise noted,
are attributed to the respective Authors or to the Holy Bible.

Cover illustration, book design and production
Copyright © 2017 by Tribute Publishing LLC
www.TributePublishing.com

"Go Forth and Make Your Life Exceptional" ™
is a copyrighted trademark of the Author, Mike Rodriguez

Scripture references are copyrighted by www.BibleGateway.com
which is operated by the Zondervan Corporation, L.L.C

Trusting in Him – Stories That Inspire

"I can do ALL THINGS through Christ who strengthens me."
Philippians 4:13

NOTES

NOTES

NOTES

www.ingramcontent.com/pod-product-compliance
Lightning Source LLC
Chambersburg PA
CBHW021128300426
44113CB00006B/332